European Film Industries

D0082631

European Film Industries

Anne Jäckel

First published in 2003 by the
BRITISH FILM INSTITUTE
21 Stephen Street, London W1T 1LN

The British Film Institute promotes greater understandings of,
and access to, film and moving image culture in the UK.

Set by Fakenham Photosetting Limited, Fakenham, Norfolk
Printed in the UK by St Edmundsbury Press, Bury St Edmunds, Suffolk

Cover design: Barefoot
Cover Illustrations: (front) Franka Potente as Lola in *Lola rennt* (*Run Lola Run*), Tom Tykwer, 1998;
(back) Emir Kusturica as the dealer in *Underground*, Emir Kusturica, 1995.

British Library Cataloguing-in-Publication Data
A catalogue record for this book is available from the British Library

ISBN 0–85170–948–6 (pbk)
ISBN–0–85170–947–8 (hbk)

Contents

Acknowledgments

Thanks to Yvon Thiec at Eurocinéma (Brussels), Richard Collins, Michel Gomez and Sylvie Monin at the ARP (Paris), David Hancock, André Lange and Lone Andersen at the European Audiovisual Observatory (Strasbourg), Ian Christie, Jean-Claude Lazaro and Anja Helm at EUROPA CINEMAS, Patrick Frater at *Screen International*, the staff at MEDIA Salles and Eurimages and at the CNC (Paris) and the EASS. The Austrian Film Commission, the Ministère de la Communauté Française de Belgique, the Dutch Ministry of Culture, Education and Science, the Danish Film Institute, the Finnish Film Foundation, the Icelandic Film Fund, the Swedish Film Institute, the Greek Film Centre, RomaniaFilm, the Czech and Polish ministries of culture and to Ruth Barton. Finally, my thanks to Dina Iordanova and Michael Wayne for insights into their publication, and the many individuals in the European film industry who have taken the time to reply to my questions/questionnaires and supply additional information.

For permission to reproduce quotes and tables: *Film Français*, CNC, EAO, EUROPA CINEMAS, MEDIA Salles.

Introduction

The film industry is unlike any other. Its products are cultural, public as well as private goods, with a symbolic (historical, national, linguistic, social) significance that cannot be reduced to a mere commodity. No other industry has similar non-economic pretensions (Hoskins *et al.*, 1997: 3). This is particularly evident in the European context. In Europe, the film industry became an international business soon after its inception (Thompson, 1985; Jarvie, 1992). More recently, Europe's position in the international film trade was brought to prominence at the Uruguay round of the General Agreement on Tariffs and Trade (GATT) in 1993 when the Europeans – led by the French – campaigned for the exclusion of film and audiovisual products from the agreement. However international the film business may be, there is a long tradition of state support, and national contexts still define industry practice and determine cultural policy in Europe. It therefore continues to make sense to discuss the importance and the competitiveness of Europe's film industries in national terms. That most countries in Europe continue to implement some form of protection for their national film industry indicates that films are considered far too socially important to be left to market forces. Any economic approach to the film business in Europe must therefore necessarily take account of the cultural priorities that are also at work in the industry.

In the past, European countries have operated policies clearly delineating between film and television. As film companies have come to increasingly rely on work and finance from the television and video sectors, so differences between film and other audiovisual products have become blurred. While there are difficulties with separating film from the other audiovisual industries, this book focuses on the industrial conditions influencing the production, distribution and exhibition of the feature film, making only occasional references to television and video where necessary. It is the intention of this study to explore the changes which have taken place in Europe's film industries, concentrating on conditions shaping those industries since the early 1990s, and to examine variations between national territories, both at the level of the industry (professional practices, the dominant players, ownership, and relationships between the various participants) and in terms of the interaction between public authorities and the film sector.

The book offers a structured examination of how the European film industries operate, analysing recent trends and discussing their implications for European public policy and business strategy. To help understand the legacy of the past on the current state of the industry in Europe, Chapter 1 gives an historical overview of how Europe's film industries developed. It also examines explanations for the US dominance of European markets. Chapter 2 explores current working practices and attitudes, investigating how these account for the distinctive characteristics of the European film industries with particular attention to labour, studios and training opportunities, as well as studio capacity, post-production facilities and the various strategies adopted in developing projects. Facilities provision largely depends on production levels. In this context, questions arise over: Which countries are the most successful? Which projects do they attract (facilitate)? What are the benefits and drawbacks of competition between studios and other production and post-production facilities within Europe? What are the opportunities and constraints for European producers today?

Systems for supporting production budgets vary greatly from one country to another. Chapter 3 examines both private sector and government (national and regional) funding sources. Who are the major film financiers today? At which level (regional, national, European or global) do they operate? How important is the role of television in film financing? Do public and private broadcasters invest in different kinds of project? What are the positive and negative aspects of government intervention? What forms does it take? How do methods of financing differ between the small and large countries? What is the situation in Central and Eastern Europe today? What forms do co-production and other co-financing partnerships take? To what extent are these responsible for a rise in film budgets? Is there a trend towards an integrated European or European–American co-financing strategy?

Chapter 4 looks at the development of European and pan-European programmes for financially supporting the film industries. To what extent have the objectives of these programmes been met? What difficulties and criticisms did these programmes encounter? Have they contributed to promoting the screening of European films outside their home territory? Some people have argued that national regulations are incompatible with European ruling. Others believe that the European Commission can only make recommendations as far as the cultural sector is concerned. Can European support mechanisms become a substitute for government intervention? Where does the power lie today in the matter of regulating Europe's film industries? Is the harmonisation of subsidies and regulations on the agenda of the European Commission? How are European and pan-European initiatives encouraging networking arrangements between producers, distributors and exhibitors from different countries? To what extent is the increasing use of international co-productions and co-ventures blurring national distinctions?

Chapters 5 and 6 examine the distribution and exhibition of film in Europe. New European and global players are rapidly emerging in the film industry. What effect does the concentrated power of these companies have on the circulation and showing of film in Europe? Do these powerful groups offer any advantage for the distribution and exhibition of European film? What developments have taken place in the distribution and exhibition sectors of Central and Eastern Europe? To what extent are existing or new players willing to endorse and/or comply with national and European legislation? How successful are European initiatives in encouraging exhibitors to show a certain proportion of European films? What is the role of film festivals today? Some territories/companies are now concentrating on export markets. Are their efforts misplaced? Should there be different strategies for selling non-English-language films? With the development of multiplex chains and the proliferation of new outlets such as video and multi-channel television, exhibition outlets for filmed entertainment have diversified, resulting in a significant increase in the total revenues of the film industry. In this context, the importance of marketing has considerably grown. What impact have these changes had on the European film industries?

These and other questions represent the core issues addressed by the following study. What follows is an analysis of present conditions in Europe's film industries. However, the production, distribution and exhibition of film in the region are constantly undergoing transformation. This study therefore not only provides perspectives from which to understand the current state of the film industries in Europe, but also to recognise the conditions that will shape those industries in the future.

I

Historical Developments in Europe's Film Industries

Historically, Europe's film industries have experienced periods of competitive strength and weakness. Rather than internal competition between nations, the main challenge facing Europe's film business has been how to maintain sustainable film industries faced with the pervasive dominance of Hollywood film. This has seen film industries become a key matter of economic and cultural policy-making among European nations. Various measures have been taken to aid or protect film in Europe, including quotas, subsidies, co-production agreements and initiatives to form pan-European distribution alliances. Tracing the history of Europe's film industries therefore involves exploring connections between market forces, conditions of cultural production, and state intervention.

THE EARLY YEARS

The early history of the film industry in Europe is one of inventors (the Lumière brothers, Max Skladanowsky, Kazimierz Proszynski) and entrepreneurs (Louis Gaumont and Charles Pathé in France, the Skladanowsky brothers and Oskar Messter in Germany and Ole Olsen, the founder of Nordisk, in Denmark). Until 1910, the majority of films distributed in the world were French. By producing and distributing films, or setting up chains of cinemas abroad, Gaumont and Pathé-Frères became powerful forces in the international film market. Early in the 20th century, other territories in Europe established film studios and began national production, Hungary in 1901, Poland in 1902 and Italy in 1905. Through the powerful cartel of the Motion Picture Patents Company, the US industry was able to restrict imports. In response, during 1909, European manufacturers made a failed attempt to form a trust in an effort to 'exercise market control and rationalise the European film industry' (Higson and Maltby, 1999: 23).[1]

World War I would strike a decisive blow to the French and other European film industries. Even before the war, the French monopoly of the film market had already ceased due to lack of investment, the failure of French companies to modernise, and strong competition from abroad (Sadoul, 1962; Thompson,

1985; Abel, 1993; Billard, 1995). Apart from Germany and its vertically integrated conglomerate Ufa, 'no European country survived World War I with a film *industry*' (Vincendeau, 1995: xiii).

INTER-WAR YEARS

World War I put an end to the global ambitions of European entrepreneurs and marked the beginning of Hollywood's domination of European markets. Two countries stood as major exceptions to this situation. A ban on supplying films to Germany meant that the national film industry there maintained its strength through producing for the domestic market. In the aftermath of the Russian revolution, cinema was nationalised under the Soviet regime. A trade blockade of the Soviet Union by the Western powers (only lifted in 1921) contributed to encourage domestic production and exhibition. Lenin famously declared, 'Of all the arts, for us cinema is the most important' (quoted in Taylor, 2000: 225) and, along with film schools, a formidable machinery for the production and distribution of propaganda films was set up.

In the West, despite intense hostility between individual nations, the 1920s saw a period of fertile development by Scandinavian, British, French, Italian and German film companies. Yet attempts at creating transnational alliances to compete with the major Hollywood studios proved elusive. Countries took protectionist measures by introducing a variety of different quota systems. Germany led the way when on 1 January 1921 it instituted the policy of restricting imports to 15 per cent of the footage produced in the country during 1919 (the equivalent of 180,000 metres) (Thompson, 1985: 106). Four years later the system was revised, with distributors being granted one import licence for every German feature they had handled in the previous year, thereby restricting foreign films to 50 per cent of the market. During the second half of the 1920s and into the 1930s, other European nations established their own systems, including Italy and Hungary in 1925, Austria in 1926, France in 1928 and Czechoslovakia in 1932 (pp. 211–12). These systems varied in how they tackled imports and were frequently revised.

Quotas aimed to protect indigenous production but in many cases they introduced problems that were to the detriment of the domestic industries. For example, in Britain, the Cinematograph Films Act of 1927 legislated that 7.5 per cent of the film footage circulated by distributors, and 5 per cent of the footage shown by exhibitors, should be of British origination (Glancy, 2000: 59). A British film was defined as a film made by a British studio, with 75 per cent of labour costs going to British citizens or citizens of the Empire, and made by a British company (defined in terms of the majority proportion of the company's directors). After the introduction of the quota, film production in Britain dramatically increased. However many of the films made were low-budget 'quota quickies', poor-quality films aimed at filling the quota (Low, 1997: 186–97). To solve this problem, the quota system was revised under the Cinematograph Films Act of 1938. While retaining the same definition of a British film, a cost test was introduced, demanding that a film should have incurred labour costs of at least £7,500 to qualify for the quota. Films with labour costs of £22,500 or £37,500 could qualify for double or triple quota credit. Rather than protect the British industry, this system was ripe for exploitation by the UK subsidiaries of the Hollywood studios. These subsidiaries were able to easily satisfy the demands of the quota, for while they were US-owned, appointment of UK citizens as company directors qualified them as British companies, and they could fulfil their annual commitment by producing three to four, double or triple quota titles that complied with the definition of British production. Mark Glancy (2000: 60) suggests this situation was particularly advantageous for the Hollywood studios at this time, as Britain was the most lucrative market in Europe for the American industry, and would become more so as the protectionist measures instituted by other nations reduced earnings from elsewhere in the region.

Collaborative agreements between private companies in the leading European film industries, and a constant flow of talent (stars, directors, costume and set designers) between Berlin, London, Paris and Rome, testified to practical co-operation between Europeans (Saunders, 1999). Cross-fertilisation occurred to such an extent that film historians have described the 1919–29 period as the 'golden' era of European cinema. In this period, a strong tradition of film art and film culture (Soviet cinema, the avant-garde, surrealism, German expressionism) developed in Europe.

Through a myriad of small companies, the major European territories managed to maintain production throughout the 1920s and 30s. In Germany, Ufa provided the only example of a powerful vertically and horizontally integrated European film conglomerate.[2] Elsewhere, small production units lacked the necessary capital to update studios and laboratories. Film personnel were therefore enticed to move to the more active centres (Ufa or Hollywood). At the beginning of the 1930s, Europe's film companies were badly affected by the Wall Street crash of 1929, and the coming of sound brought a further blow to film industries lacking the necessary resources to invest in the new technology. American (Paramount) and German (Tobis) companies established several partnerships with European studios (Berlin, Joinville, Epinay) in order to make multiple-language versions, but the trend did not last. With some countries (France, Germany), however, the decade did represent a golden age for domestic popular cinema (Martin, 1983).

World War II brought mixed consequences for the domestic film industries of Europe. While many individuals went into exile, a new generation of film-makers managed to emerge. In the case of France, occupation saw the country inherit an effective organisational framework for the activities of its film industry with the formation of the Comité d'Organisation des Industries Cinéma-tographiques (COIC).[3] German occupation also saw a ban on Hollywood films in the major markets of continental Europe. After the war, the huge stockpile of unreleased American productions entered European cinemas on the tails of the Marshall Plan. As this surge of US imports came at a time of great audience demand, when national cinema infrastructures needed rebuilding, European film professionals mounted concerted protests to protect their domestic indus-tries (Jeancolas, 1992).

POST-WAR DEVELOPMENTS IN THE WEST

To combat the flood of US imports, governments implemented protective measures (quotas, subsidies and tax incentives) in support of their domestic industries.[4] Some of these measures (e.g. freezing American assets) resulted in Hollywood companies setting up subsidiaries in Europe in order to take advan-tage of local incentives for film production (Guback, 1969). In Britain, where MGM, Columbia and Fox established studio facilities to produce films, one-third of 'British' films had US backing by 1956. Various attempts at creating a European cinema union in the post-war era failed. However, collaboration between producers from different countries flourished under the aegis of inter-governmental co-production agreements.

CASE STUDY: THE CO-PRODUCTION AGREEMENT BETWEEN FRANCE AND ITALY

Frenchman M. Fourré-Cormeray is credited with the idea of a treaty giving film dual nationality. After making an experimental co-production agreement in 1946, the governments of France and Italy responded to pressure from their domestic industries by signing the 1949 Franco-Italian Agreement. It was the aim of the Agreement to return production to pre-war levels and, by making 'quality films', compete on the international market and offset the domination of Hollywood (Jäckel, 1996). Co-production status was granted to films with equal financial, artistic and technical contributions, as well as to 'twinned' films (that is, films in pairs with complementary participation from each co-producer). It was stipulated that an Italian–French Mixed Committee meet regularly to supervise the functioning of the agreement.

The agreement supported a range of complex and contradictory objectives: pooling resources together, opening the domestic markets of both countries to co-productions, determining the eligibility of co-productions for national subsidies and other benefits such as screen quotas, and encouraging the production of prestigious films appealing to both domestic and international audiences. Not all went well between co-production partners. Employment issues, such as apportioning the nationality of technicians being employed, and which nation's studios were to be used, were constant subjects of discord between Italian and French unions. Other disadvantages seemingly inherent in the system (cost escalation, differences in investment levels, compromises concerning the creative talent and the kind of films made) also emerged.

However, despite all those drawbacks, by 1953–4 the principal aims of the treaty were fulfilled. The Italian and French film industries had substantially increased their volume of production, and employment figures had risen. In terms of quality (e.g. star appeal and technical innovation), French–Italian films ranked high: co-productions made the launching of international stars possible and, compared to non-co-productions, more were made in colour (*ibid.*). Several French–Italian films also won critical acclaim and prizes at film festivals around the world. Examples include *Au-delà des grilles* (*Mura di Malapaga*) (René Clément 1949) and *Nous sommes tous des assassins* (*Are We All Murderers?*) (André Cayatte 1952) at Cannes; and *Touchez pas au grisbi* (*Honour Among Thieves*) (Jacques Becker 1954) at Venice.

Thérèse Raquin (*The Adulteress*, 1953)

Other countries made similar agreements. By the mid-1950s, France had co-production agreements with Germany, Spain, Argentina, Austria, Yugoslavia, Australia and the Soviet Union. Italy formed alliances with the German Federal Republic, Spain and Argentina. (The Netherlands, Sweden, Denmark and Hungary would also sign co-production agreements in the 50s.) However, by then, a significant number of films were already made with the participation of one or several foreign companies from countries that had not signed an agreement but that nevertheless benefited from the aid granted by national governments, pro-rata of their investment in the country. Designed to encourage production, the system had inevitably started to attract foreign (largely American but also British) producers eager to take advantage of the financial incentives offered by the governments of France and Italy. With the authorities often turning a blind eye to the penetration of foreign capital and personnel, Italian studios soon became service studios for wealthy, expatriate American producers.

Regularly revised – more often to allow flexibility between partners than to strictly enforce nationality criteria – for the next fifty years the Franco-Italian agreement became a model in Europe and beyond for countries seeking to secure a sustained production output.

POST-WAR DEVELOPMENTS IN THE EAST

In the post-war period, the Communist regimes of the Eastern Bloc (with the exception of Albania) made a strong commitment to supporting their film industries, as well as film education, even in periods of economic crisis. The USSR established a Ministry of Cinematography in 1946. Poland restructured and nationalised its film industry in 1945, and Film Polski was set up as a leading production house. In Czechoslovakia, the Prague film school FAMU was founded in 1947 and a separate Slovak cinema was established with its own studios at Loliba in Bratislava. In 1948, Hungary and Romania both nationalised their film industries. The I. L. Caragiale Institute of Theatre and Film Art was founded in Bucharest in 1950, and between 1952 and 1958, the Buftea studios were built. Known as 'the Cinecittà of South-Eastern Europe', the Romanian studios were the centre of a highly centralised film industry. With some of the largest sound stages in Europe, a wide range of impressive permanent sets, and good-quality European equipment, the Buftea studios attracted productions from all over Europe.

Under a state-controlled system, domestic production in Eastern European countries during the late 1940s and early 50s was marked by Party ideology. Following Stalin's death (1953) and Khrushchev's de-Stanilisation speech of 1956, a limited political thaw set in allowing a significant restructuring of film production and giving film-makers greater artistic control.

CHANGES AND NEW TRENDS FROM THE LATE 1950s ONWARDS

In the East and the West during the late 1950s, a fresh generation of film-makers started to emerge, injecting new life into the film industry. Formulated by the young French director, François Truffaut in *Cahiers du cinéma* in 1954, the *politique des auteurs*, argued for the director having artistic responsibility for a film, and contributed to raising the status of a number of film-makers. Yet the individual style and freer approach of the French New Wave owed as much to new techniques (hand-held cameras) and the introduction of measures to help young film-makers as to a desire to rebel against the film practices of the period.[5] Other changes in the socio-economic climate also promoted the rise of the New Wave. A fast-growing economy, new cultural attitudes (an emerging consumer mentality, sexual awareness)[6] and problems encountered by Hollywood (inflexible structures of the studio system, high production costs, competition from television) created openings for European film production. Offering more financial incentives and greater flexibility, Italy proved more attractive than France as a centre for film production. Several producers (Dino de Laurentiis, Carlo Ponti) began to emerge as prominent figures in European film-making. Indifferent to quotas and other regulations, they invested in both large-scale spectacular films and auteur films (Gili and Tassone, 1995).

The period was seen as another 'Golden Age' for European cinema. Both the Cannes and Venice film festivals became important showcases for European films. The cinematic culture that had blossomed with the development of *art et essai* cinemas and the emergence of new *cinéphile* magazines was enlivened by the talent of the New Wave film-makers. For a short period, the intersection of trends on both sides of the Atlantic (European directors who admired Hollywood movies and American interests spurred by the novelty and sophistication of the films of European auteurs) brought what Peter Lev (1993) aptly called 'the Euro-American art film'. However, in the long term, it also led to its downfall. Even before the so-called 'American runaway productions' returned home, there were already signs that several years of over-production and inflated costs had taken their toll. By 1964, much of the Italian film industry was in financial difficulties (Crisp, 1994).

Following a steady increase after World War II, from the 1950s cinema admissions began to decline as television became popular. Many governments (Austria, Belgium, Denmark, Finland, France, Ireland and Spain) introduced requirements for television broadcasters – most under state ownership – to undertake a programme of support for their domestic film industry, with obligations to co-produce a certain number of films, and restrictions on the number of films shown on television. In the long run, television support would become crucial to the survival of the European film industries.

In the late 1960s, the major Hollywood studios, under pressure from American unions, started to move their assets back home. By the mid-70s, national policies changed as the international economy soured in the wake of the oil crises. While government regulatory powers remained or became more persuasive in some countries (e.g. requiring national television stations to contribute to the production of films for the cinema), in others the film industry followed a market model. With the major exception of Germany, the 1970s were an unremarkable period for Europe's cinema industries. A steady diet of comedies, political thrillers (Italy, France), horror films (Britain) and pornographic movies became standard.

Despite political censorship, in the Eastern Bloc the 1960s, 70s and even the 80s saw an impressive output of critically significant films. Examples include *Reconstituirea* (*Reconstitution*) (Lucian Pintilie 1969 Romania), *Andrei Rublëv* (Andrei Tarkovsky 1966 USSR), *Czlowiek z Marmur* (*Man of Marble*) (Andrzej Wajda 1976 Poland). This international recognition helped several controversial film-makers to be 'tolerated' by governments only too happy to welcome extra foreign income. As Daniel Goulding (1998: 476) points out, the emergence of these films

> raised serious issues concerning the subtle and complex interrelationships of politics, art, and social commitment within a government-subsidized system of film production, distribution and exhibition [and raised questions] of artistic freedom, censorship, and the economic and ideological determinants of artistic production.

Czlowiek z Marmur (*Man of Marble*, 1976)

ATTEMPTS AT PAN-EUROPEAN DISTRIBUTION

Attempts at forging pan-European distribution operations go back to the earliest decades of cinema. During the 1920s, a series of film congresses – most notably the 1926 Paris Conference – were dedicated to establishing pan-European collaboration in film production and distribution. Often considered a precursor of today's European film policies, the resulting 'Film Europe' movement 'describe[d] the ideal of a vibrant pan-European cinema industry, making international co-productions for a massively enhanced "domestic" market ... challeng[ing] American distributors for control of that market ... [but] always existed more as a set of principles than concrete practices' (Higson and Maltby, 1999: 2). However, some of the leading German, French and British companies of the time did adopt 'loosely related industrial policies which were designed to be of mutual benefit' (p. 2). That these efforts failed had much to do with the aftermath of World War I and the inability of Europeans to organise and set up a common trade association to compete with the powerful Motion Picture Producers and Distributors of America Inc. (Thompson, 1985). The Depression, the impact of sound, and the rise of nationalist movements in Europe would also hamper such attempts.

The idea of a pan-European cinema did not die. Martin Dale (1997: 158) recalls the debates from the 1960s when 'several high-level conferences concentrated on the need for pan-European distributors to fill the gap left by the Hollywood Majors'. At the time, industry analyst Jean-Claude Batz explained the reasons why distribution had been 'the black hole' in the systems of state support for the cinema.

> [T]his omission is not as surprising as it first seems. It is due to the fact that distribution only has sense when structured on an international level, or at least across several territories, which means that governments realize that they would be unable to control such companies, because their activities go beyond the state's narrow frontiers (quoted in Dale, 1997: 158).[7]

Ten years later, French giant Gaumont, under the leadership of Daniel Toscan du Plantier, attempted to establish such a network with a cross-border operation in Italy. Established in 1978, the Gaumont-Italia experiment failed in its ambitions, and operations closed after only a few years (Garçon, 1995).

The 1980s witnessed a major attempt to set up a pan-European consortium with the Eurotrustees venture. Founded by a group of distributors including Palace Pictures in the UK, Bac Films in France, Iberoamericana in Spain, Concorde in Germany and ERRE in Italy, Eurotrustees was backed by the UK bank Guinness Mahon and Dutch bank Pierson & Heldring. 'The aim was to decide jointly on projects and each partner put up a minimum guarantee which would represent an equity stake on the entire global revenues, rather than a stake in a specific territory' (Dale, 1997: 158). By acquiring rights on a group basis, the partners hoped to be able to exercise much greater power in the marketplace when competing for product, and to co-ordinate distribution strategies across different territories to maximise profit potential. By pooling financial resources, they also hoped to pre-buy or buy pictures at an earlier stage in a film's life cycle. However, bringing together companies with their own distinctive identities and strategies took a long time. Reaching agreement on a particular project also proved difficult. Shortly after Eurotrustees decided to back Neil Jordan's *The Crying Game* (1992 UK/JP), the venture collapsed when Palace went bankrupt. That the whole project could be brought down by the downfall of just one of five participants underlines the fragility of federations formed between independents.

EUROPE VERSUS HOLLYWOOD

Distribution in Europe is dominated by the international divisions of the major Hollywood studios: United International Pictures (UIP, the international distribution operation of Paramount and Universal Pictures), Columbia TriStar (the international distribution division of Sony Pictures Entertainment), 20th Century-Fox and Warner Bros. The Walt Disney Company has released its own pictures in most European territories through Buena Vista International, its overseas distribution operation.

In the past, Europe's few vertically integrated groups (Bertelsmann, Gaumont, Pathé, UGC, Rank, Canon) had distribution arms to exploit their own productions in the domestic market (Dale, 1997). In the 1980s, European distributors responded to the Hollywood majors by forging closer links with European production companies and broadcasters, or by forming alliances with financial institutions to provide funds for the acquisition of rights from the majors. European companies have also negotiated deals with American companies, and the most successful distributors have been those that have also distributed US films (Coopers & Lybrand, 1991).

During the 1980s, while Europeans were considering the merits of European unification and debating the advantages or disadvantages of protection and deregulation for their audiovisual industries (e.g. the controversial Television without Frontiers Directive or TWFD), the US majors won over European audiences with their massively promoted blockbusters. The Hollywood studios continued to show enormous flexibility in adapting to change by investing in multiplexes, new delivery technologies (pay television, video, Internet) and independent production outlets.

American omnipresence was behind European (particularly French) protests to obtain the exclusion of films and audiovisual programmes from the General Agreement on Tariffs and Trade (GATT) in 1993. In the name of free trade and consumer sovereignty, the American representatives sought to stop EC subsidies and quotas. At the time, European protests against the American dominance of the film trade were largely argued in terms of US imperialism. Protestors denounced the persistent and aggressive lobbying by the Motion Picture Association of America (MPAA) to promote the interests of the American film industry while 'ensuring European films would not enter the American market'.[8]

Several other economic, social and cultural factors are frequently identified to explain the competitive advantage of the US over the European film industries:

- the existence of a large and wealthy home market (Wildman and Siwek, 1988; Hoskins and McFadyen, 1991)
- Hollywood's attraction of European talent
- the ubiquity of – and fascination for – of all things American, and of American advertising and consumer products in particular (Guback, 1969; Tunstall, 1977; Sorlin, 1992)
- the insularity of American audiences
- the prevalence of the English language (Collins, 1989)

More recent factors explaining US success include huge promotion budgets, the development of multiplexes and new technologies, together with the increased importance of foreign markets for the Hollywood studios.

In contrast with the majors' business approach to film and their ability to adapt to economic, socio-cultural and technological change, European cinema is associated with auteurism, or the celebration of the director as artist. Quoting Jean-Luc Godard saying 'film is only made for one or two people', David Puttnam argues Europe's attitude to 'film as art' is ultimately self-destructive:

> [The auteur theory] rapidly mutated into a political ideology which played a key role in shaping both the aesthetics and economics of European film-making for twenty-five years or more. In doing so, it seems as if it has condemned much of Europe's cinema to a cultural ghetto from which it may never have the will to escape (Puttnam and Watson, 1997: 303).

This line of criticism, largely coming from UK commentators (Finney, 1996; Ilott, 1996; Dale, 1997; Puttnam and Watson, 1997), usually argues European cinema has fallen foul of

- a certain 'subsidy mentality' believed to create non-commercial, non-competitive productions
- misdirected and/or inadequate protectionist measures at European level
- little attention to the development phase of film-making
- a lack of investment in distribution and marketing

Yet, as a British reviewer of Puttnam's book, *The Undeclared War*, pointed out in 1999:

> Puttnam's anti-European strictures would be rather more convincing and palatable if relatively subsidy-free Britain had succeeded where our continental neighbours have allegedly failed. However, the incontrovertible fact is that, thanks to subsidy, other forms of state intervention, and a conception of cinema that embraces culture as well as commerce, France has a film industry, and we have what Ian Christie has called a 'precarious network of boutique producers' and 'more a carefully contrived illusion than a serious industry' (Petley, 1999: 171).[9]

In Europe, the campaign leading to the December 1993 decision to temporarily exclude cultural products from the GATT highlighted divisions between partisans of liberal and *dirigiste* approaches (Collins, 1994). Four years earlier, the European Union's MEDIA programme (Mesures pour Encourager le Développement de l'Industrie Audiovisuelle) and the Council of Europe's Eurimages initiative, had been created to help establish European networks of co-operation and exchange with the aim of mobilising capital resources through partnerships in the audiovisual industries. By the Uruguay round of GATT, the founders of Eurimages had seen their hope that co-productions would accelerate the process of European unification, fail to materialise. If the pan-European initiatives effectively encouraged production (the number of co-productions largely increased and, in some countries, the number of national productions also rose), the distribution and the appreciation of European films beyond their national borders had not significantly improved.

A NEW SITUATION IN CENTRAL AND EASTERN EUROPE

In Central and Eastern Europe, mass regular cinemagoing started to decline in the 1980s in the wake of *Perestroika*. Even more dramatic were the changes to the former Eastern Bloc's film industries which followed the fall of the Berlin wall in 1989:

> The shift to a market economy affected every level of the film industry from its basic infrastructure to its mode of financing and administration. The pattern of

changes in the media economy and film industries was similar throughout all East European countries: a sharp decrease in state funding, empty studios looking to attract foreign crews, the disappearance of domestic films from the circuits, armies of idle film professionals, and the redefinition of concepts like 'copyrights', 'entertainment' and 'audience' (Wood and Iordanova, 2000: 2).

Reflecting on the situation of Soviet and Eastern European film-makers in 1990, Graham Petrie and Ruth Dwyer (1990: 5) asked: 'is there any place any longer, even in Poland, Hungary and Czechoslovakia, for films that put artistic require- ments ahead of commercial ones?' They added: 'all these countries, and even the Soviet Union, need desperately to sell their films abroad if their industries are to survive'. This point is also valid for the film industries of the West, where national and European initiatives are now moving towards a more commercially driven approach.

CONCLUSION

Europe's film industries have long fought to establish, maintain and revive their place in the international film business. Responding to competition from outside the region, especially from Hollywood, European nations have introduced quo- tas, subsidies and co-production agreements to protect, promote or expand their film industries. Both competition and collaboration have always existed on a glo- bal scale in the film world. Hollywood has invested in Europe and vice versa. In Europe, countries with similar institutions and cultural affinities, such as France and Italy, or the Scandinavian countries, have a long and successful tradition of co-production. The Nordic countries (Denmark, Finland, Iceland, Norway and Sweden) have established specific joint organisations, such as the Nordic Film and Television Fund, to provide sustained co-operation, and pan-Scandinavian co-production is almost second nature to the leading Danish, Swedish and Norwegian production companies. Producers from countries that share a com- mon language (Belgium/France/Switzerland, Austria/Germany/Switzerland, Ire- land/UK) also tend to work in partnership. Co-productions constitute an activity without which many small countries would not have a film industry.

The power of European film industries in the global film market has experi- enced many historical fluctuations. Electronic and digital technologies are now creating new opportunities but also having unsettling effects for the film indus- tries. Yet uncertainty is nothing new. Interrelationships between the functions of production, distribution and exhibition have always been extremely complex and constantly changing. One thing, however, remains constant: the companies and individuals performing those functions constitute an essential and dynamic foundation for the sector. Working practices, the promotion of industry training schemes, and the role of producers, will therefore be among the matters discussed in the next chapter.

NOTES

1. European manufacturers organised a series of meetings, the most important of which was the European Convention held in Paris in 1909.
2. Ufa was indirectly taken over by the German state in the late 1930s and, in the early 40s, the German film industry (consolidated into Ufa) came under direct control of the Ministry of Propaganda.
3. In the early 1940s, the German administration, under the leadership of Greven (a former film producer for Ufa) and in consultation with the French authorities, established the COIC to monitor and control film production and distribution in occupied France. Films, like people, were subjected to successive controls: production, exhibition and export visas were required. Exhibitors became accountable for keeping records of receipts for each screening. As Colin Crisp (1994: 52) pointed out, 'reliable knowledge concerning the success or failure of particular films, genres, cinemas, regions and the industry as a whole became available from this time onwards'.
4. After the collapse of the Nazi regime, Germany was the only European territory where American interests were able to penetrate distribution and exhibition virtually without obstacle.
5. In 1953, the Centre National de la Cinématographie (CNC) introduced new measures to supplement the 1948 Film Aid. Also known as the Paris Agreement, the 1948 Film Aid replaced the Blum-Byrnes Agreement: it increased screen quotas from four to five weeks during each quarter and resurrected import quotas (186 dubbed films, 121 of which could be American) (Guback, 1969: 22). A new development fund for the film industry (FDIC) provided selective aid to short films and quality films. Although negligible in financial terms, the fund contributed to the emergence of new talent.
6. As Peter Lev points out, the impact of films such as Vadim's *Et Dieu ... créa la femme* (*And God Created Woman*) (1956 France) on the film industry was significant. 'Explicit sexuality became expected in foreign films, to such an extent that, "foreign film", "art film", "adult film" and "sex film" were for several years almost synonyms' (Lev, 1993: 13).
7. Also see Batz and Degand (1968).
8. Statement made in several speeches by Jacques Toubon, France's Minister of Culture in 1993.
9. Quoted comment from Christie (1997). The British government has now set up a Film Council whose task is to develop a sustainable UK film industry and enhance film and moving image culture and education (Film Council, 2000: 3).

2

Developing and Facilitating Production

Film production necessitates the bringing together of an enormous array of different trades, skills, aptitudes and sensitivities under coordinated managerial and aesthetic control. Any single project entails not just the raising of funds and overall program management but also calls into play the tasks of (a) pre-production (e.g. scenario development, casting, set and costume design), (b) shooting (e.g. camera-work, lighting, acting, make-up), (c) post-production (e.g. editing, special effects, sound engineering). In addition, needed equipment and studio space must be found and rented (Allen J. Scott, 2000b: 17–18).

This chapter examines conditions affecting production in Europe's film industries. It examines current working practices and investigates how they account for the well-known peculiarities found in European cinema. It also looks at the facilitating of film-making through studio and post-production resources. Operating strategies and constraints are explored, together with the importance of promoting development and training as vital to building and sustaining the health of the industry. Finally, the chapter looks at the role of producers, considering how the context of European film production has demanded the balancing of creative and business objectives.

WORKING PRACTICES IN THE EUROPEAN FILM INDUSTRY
Employment and Heterogeneity in the Sector

Film production is a growing but high-risk industry. Most professionals involved in the sector do not rely solely on film to provide them with employment. Theatre, television, advertising and related industries provide other employment opportunities for film workers. Extreme volatility in the sector makes it impossible to put a figure on the number of film producers active in any particular year. In France, for instance, a *Screen Digest* survey (1999b: 265) identified 157 production companies and 279 facilities companies active in 1998. This is far below the figures given by the Centre National de la Cinématographie (CNC) (May 2000: 78) for the previous year: their records show 5,657 companies working in the audiovisual sector, 'in the broadest possible sense', of which 725 were production companies (cinema), 807 production companies (television) and 1,308 production facilities (see also Benhamou [1997] and Greffe [1997]).

In Eastern Europe, the industry still largely comprises small production companies working in conjunction with existing studios on a film-by-film basis. In the West, where the number of mergers and alliances has increased, groups of individuals and firms still most often come together on an ad hoc temporary basis (Allen J. Scott, 2000b: 18). Studies of the French film industry – the most regulated in Europe – show that two-thirds of all work in the French film industry is on a temporary basis and that workers are subject to frequent periods of unemployment (CNC, 1997; Allen J. Scott, 2000b).

Labour Costs and Working Practices

Working practices in the film industry are often subject to individual negotiations and are therefore not always transparent. These practices differ widely between countries and individual projects. Labour costs are also a politically sensitive factor in attracting foreign companies. It is therefore difficult to arrive at any clear evaluation of labour costs for film crews across European territories.

To date, the only attempt at comparing production costs across EU countries is the research done in 1998 by France's Association des Réalisateurs et Producteurs (ARP).[1] This study identified and measured the main reasons for production costs differentials on the same types of film across France, Germany, Italy, Spain and the UK. In the first stage, the research defined below-the-line production costs (technical expenses and labour) for three French films of differing budget sizes (type A – budget under FF7 or 8 million; type B – budgeted around FF18 million; and type C – around FF50 million).[2] The second stage consisted of collecting data on similar types of film by directors or producers from the other four EU territories. Finally, the research compared the production costs in France with those of the other countries and made recommendations for France regarding working practices. The study was based on national films. It did not take into account overseas, notably US, productions shooting in Europe. As a result, it did not include high-budget films from the UK, as these tended to be US-financed projects. Data from Spain was based solely on comparisons between low-budget and medium-budget films since there were practically no high-budget productions at that time.

What the study showed was that average labour costs per week were widely divergent between European territories. Of the five countries studied, the UK was the country with the highest rates of pay and the narrowest range of salaries. France and Germany also had a fairly narrow range of salaries. Both Spain and

Italy showed large salary differences between managers and workers. France had the highest labour costs, explained by

- a narrow range of salaries
- a shorter working week and overtime payments
- generous transport allowances and food provision
- high levels of 'social charges' (employers' and NI contributions) (52 per cent)

Differences in legislation across the European Union accounted for wide divergence between the social charges made in the five countries studied. The UK claimed the lowest social charges (10.23 per cent) with the system encouraging self-employment. The complexity of the systems in Italy and Spain justified the employment of an administrator during the shoot to handle these matters alone.

On working practices, the study also uncovered a number of variations between the countries, including

- a higher level of preparation before a shoot in the UK
- larger crews in the UK (due to a high degree of specialisation)
- a large administrative staff in Italy, Germany and Spain
- the greater use of post-synchronisation in Italy and Spain
- a higher level of social protection in France

Along with these practical variations, all five countries had very different film economies and competitive strengths:

- the lowest overall labour costs in Spain
- the most versatile shoot teams in Germany and Italy
- a high level of technical development and good organisational framework in the UK
- a wide diversity of production and post-production facilities in France and the UK

Identifying the strengths and weaknesses of the five major EU territories, in summary the authors of the report commented:

> It is not our purpose to define a model and to attempt to conform to it, nor to define the ideal country as this would result in proposals combining: UK rationale for industrialisation with Italian flexibility, a Spanish sense of responsibility and resourcefulness with British [low] social charges, Spanish [long] working hours

worked in British studios, German locations, French creativity and speediness, Spanish horses and extras... (author's translation, ARP, 1998: 25–6).

On the technological level, the ARP study reported that the five countries had been, or were in the process of, re-equipping their industries (with Italy still lagging behind), and digital non-linear editing was gaining currency all over Europe. It emphasised the fact that the competitive environment of the European film industries was getting harsher and saw critical mass and/or volume activity as the key to success for the technical industries (pp. 28–9).

STUDIOS

Film studios serve a variety of different media industries, including film and television production, photography and advertising. In the whole of Europe, studio fortunes have picked up again largely due to rising demand by television producers and increased levels of feature film production in the EU over the last decade (see Chapter 3).

Western Europe

Along with the most efficient organisational framework, the UK has the highest studio capacity in Europe. In the late 1990s, it was mainly American money that filled British studios with the bigger productions, such as *Star Wars: Episode I – The Phantom Menace* (George Lucas 1999 US), *Saving Private Ryan* (Steven Spielberg 1998 US), *Mission: Impossible II* (John Woo 2000 US/Germany) and *102 Dalmatians* (Kevin Lima 2000 US). At the beginning of 2001, the Office of Fair Trading cleared the merger of the UK's two largest film and television studios, Pinewood and Shepperton. With a management team headed by the directing brothers Tony and Ridley Scott (who acquired Pinewood in 1995 in partnership with a group of American investors), together with the former Channel 4 executive Michael Grade, the studio hoped to create a global rival to Hollywood.

After the UK, Germany and France have the highest studio capacity. Describing the agglomeration of film studios around Paris, Allen J. Scott (2000a) writes:

> Most studios are nowadays highly specialised on the leasing out of sound stages, but some, especially larger studios in suburban locations, may offer additional services such as carpentry for set construction, equipment rental, or post-production work, on either a vertically integrated or an inside contracting basis. A few studios have come to be nuclei of small clusters of independent technical industries, but there is nothing in France to compare with the sizable agglomerations [...] around the Pinewood and especially the Shepperton studios outside London (pp. 102–3).

In the late 1990s, difficulties encountered in finding a buyer for the former state-owned studio SFP, and protests by industry workers, illustrate the problems faced by the French government when attempting to privatise what was regarded as a national asset.

Looking at centres of production activity in Europe at the end of the 1990s, *Screen Digest* (1999b: 265–7) found that in France and England, film production was heavily concentrated around the capital. In France, for example, 91 per cent of production companies were concentrated around Paris. By contrast, production companies in Germany were more geographically dispersed, 'with Berlin accounting for 28 per cent, Munich for 40 per cent and Hamburg just under 10 per cent' (p. 265). Germany and the UK, and to a lesser extent France, were found to be at the forefront in offering post-production facilities, while Italy and Spain suffered from the common perception that they lacked modern equipment and studio space. Cinecittà provided the Italian industry with sufficient studio space, but in recent years had struggled to attract major foreign productions for shooting and post-production work (p. 267).

Efforts to improve existing facilities and/or build new ones are not limited to the larger countries of Europe. Small territories like Denmark, Ireland and Luxembourg have a high studio capacity for their size. In the case of Luxembourg, the presence of a major audiovisual group (CLT-Ufa) strengthened the country's position in Europe's media economy, and the new studio Delux Productions attracted North American and European talent. In Austria, the Rosenhügel film studios have been turned into a real Medienpark, with over twenty companies offering services (costumes, sets, make-up, special effects, editing, dubbing, etc.) in an effort to compete with neighbouring German, Czech and Slovak facilities.

Even though facilities provision has benefited from growth in film and television production levels, few studios can rely solely on domestic productions. As a result of competition for international productions, there have been signs of polarisation of film production around those territories with a mix of high studio capacity, tax benefits and an advanced post-production infrastructure (*Screen Digest*, 1999b). In the EU, the most successful territories at attracting foreign (non-EU) companies are, not surprisingly, the two English-language countries (UK and Ireland), Germany (where there is no restriction on shooting in English) and, to a lesser extent, Luxembourg and Denmark. For studios and post-production facilities in those countries and parts of Central and Eastern Europe (see below), the renaissance witnessed in the 1990s was partly driven by US productions coming to Europe. While outside productions may attract revenue and introduce expertise, enabling the parallel development of indigenous industries, they do not provide medium- or long-term security. This explains why many in the European film business tend to share the view of an Irish industry veteran when he said, after the introduction of Tax Law Section 35 triggered a boom in studio work in his country, that 'Ireland is in favour [with foreign producers] at the moment but I've been too involved with up-and-down activity to regard this as a boom' (see Duncan, 1995).[3]

Central and Eastern Europe

When the Berlin wall came down, many industry professionals in the West feared that studio work would be lured to the expansive and inexpensive facilities of Central and Eastern Europe. Low labour costs and favourable exchange rates seemed to give the film industries of these countries a serious competitive advantage. However, despite the interest shown by Westerners, studios throughout the region have not found it easy to make the transition to capitalism, and several are now struggling. When studios manage to survive, it is mainly through television work for national and foreign companies. With maintenance budgets reduced to the bare minimum and running on dated equipment, privatisation efforts have so far not brought about the boom forecast in the early 1990s.

Studios in Central and Eastern Europe continue to attract the more ambitious foreign productions, particularly those requiring large casts of costumed extras. Local actors, technicians and locations have also been used by some of the larger American and European productions. Steven Spielberg

Underground (1995)

shot *Schindler's List* (1993 US) on location in Poland. Bernardo Bertolucci used some of the Boyana studio facilities in Bulgaria to shoot *Little Buddha* (1993 UK/France). Emir Kusturica's *Underground* (1995 France/Germany/ Hungary) provided temporary employment to many unemployed Bulgarian workers from Plovdiv's bankrupt metal plant (Iordanova, 2002a). In 1995, Rafaella de Laurentiis' production of *Dragonheart* (Rob Cohen 1996 US) occupied all three studios at the Koliba production facility in Slovakia. *Nostradamus* (Roger Christian 1994 UK/Germany) and *Capitaine Conan* (1996 France), Bertrand Tavernier's post-World War I drama set in the Balkans, were both shot in Romania. The country also provided a location during 2001 for Costa-Gavras' *Amen* (*Eyewitness*) (2002 France/Germany). *Mission: Impossible* (Brian de Palma 1996 US) and Nikita Mikhalkov's Russian epic *Sibirskij Tsiryulnik* (*The Barber of Siberia*) (1999 France/Russia/Italy/Czech Republic) were shot at the Barrandov studios in the Czech Republic. Production of Luc Besson's *Joan of Arc* (1999 France) during 1998 saw the construction of a medieval town – complete with a bridge – in the Czech Republic by Prague International Films (Gaumont's Czech representative). Four hundred local people were reported to have worked on the set and an even larger number as extras on the film.

For such films, these countries offer the best value for money. However, the attractiveness of these facilities mean that studios must actively compete for Western productions. Poland (a location for *Schindler's List* and *The Ogre* [Volker Schlöndorff 1996 France/Germany/UK]), the Czech Republic (its Barrandov studios claiming the largest studio space in Europe),[4] Slovakia (with the Koliba studios in the capital Bratislava) and Hungary (the Mafilm studio in Budapest) have been the most successful countries at attracting productions to the East. Elsewhere in the region, studios have faced significant financial and managerial problems. Foreign productions may have helped pay bills and maintain some of the staff, but opinion differs on whether competition has either encouraged film industries in the region to expand or has pushed the industry to the verge of extinction.

STRATEGIES AND CONSTRAINTS

The next part of this chapter will explore European producers' strategies and constraints in the present environment.

De-localisation

Competitiveness in the film industry is not simply a matter of labour costs. As the success of countries with higher labour costs shows (e.g. France, UK), many other factors need to be taken into account. Labour market flexibility is just as important as government charges on labour. Quality of personnel, level of studio infrastructure, and standards of production or post-production facilities are other significant factors. Film policies (domestic and foreign) can play a significant role in helping rescue or develop a film industry. Political circumstances (e.g. in the former Yugoslavia), language and other social and cultural differences, also prove to be important in determining decisions concerning shooting a film in a particular territory. Local tax incentives, an advantageous legal framework (e.g. Ireland, Luxembourg, Portugal, Hungary), attractive locations, opportunistic behaviour and networking opportunities (Creton, 1997; Feigelson, 2000) equally count as important criteria for 'de-localisation', that is, moving production to foreign territories in order to take advantage of the benefits they offer.

Networking

Network arrangements seem particularly well suited to the specificities of Europe's variegated film industries. Access to a networked structure helps achieve economies of scale and does not necessarily require equal resources to be made available to all partners. The success of the network depends on its capacity to develop coherent strategies and to manage a complex and sophisticated structure based on complementary and convergent interests (Creton, 1994). As competition intensifies, joint agreements are becoming more common between Europeans, with producers and facilities providers making alliances to form vertical and horizontal integration strategies.

CASE STUDY: THE MAX VENTURE

Started in 1999, the Max European Post-production Alliance seemed to offer a good example of a Europe-wide strategy of co-operation aimed at reducing the uncertainty of the business. In the late 1990s, large-scale special effects and image processing capabilities were still relatively scarce in Europe, representing a trendy niche market into which several companies were eager to enter in spite of the costly technical equipment required. Initially the Max project brought together post-production facilities from four countries: Germany (Das Werk), France (Mikros Image), Italy (Blue Gold) and Belgium (ACE Editing Facilities). Combining the respective talents of several smaller companies into one entity, the project aimed to attract post-production work on ambitious productions.

However, this pan-European alliance constituted 'a direct challenge to the larger facilities companies, especially those working in Britain and Germany, in order to attract lucrative US major projects and the larger European projects' (*Screen Digest*, 1999b: 266). Moreover, each entity did not stand still. Within a year and a half, the German partner, having acquired spending capital through a flotation on Frankfurt's Neuer Markt, had become Europe's strongest post-production entity after a series of acquisitions in Germany, Portugal and Spain. By the end of 2000, Das Werk had a strong foothold in the US and was planning to develop further its position in America. In the meantime, the French company Mikros was forging alliances with other French post-production outfits (Monteurs' Studio and Merjithur). The Max venture illustrates the extent to which post-production companies felt the need to adapt to a rapidly changing world and remain competitive. The rise of Das Werk to the status of 'a post-production major' also shows that the ambitions of the largest European players were not aimed only at Europe but at the world market as well.

Specialisation and Innovation

Over the last few years, the output of European producers has displayed degrees of specialisation and innovation in particular areas of film-making. Animation is one field of production where European producers have made their mark. The Czech Republic has a long-standing reputation for animation, but the UK, France, Germany, Denmark and Ireland are moving into the field. Aardman Animation in the UK now enjoys worldwide success with the company's short and feature-length films. Aardman's deal with DreamWorks SKG, the Hollywood studio formed in 1994, is a rare example whereby a US studio invests (reportedly US$250 million) to help build up a major European-based animation facility while giving 'a significant degree of creative independence' to the European company (Pennington, 2000). However, following the success of *Toy Story* (John Lasseter 1995 US), it was Spain, not the UK, which produced the first European 3D animation feature film. Supported by the region of Galicia, the Spanish Ministry of Culture and MEDIA II, the film *El bosque animado* (Manolo Gómez and Ángel de la Cruz 2001 Spain) benefited from pre-sales to Spanish broadcasters and to Disney's international distribution division, Buena Vista International. European collaboration is also taking place in the animation sector. Both Germany and Ireland have targeted animation as a possible area of specialisation, sometimes co-producing together.

Special effects is another area in which several European studios and post-production houses are trying to establish themselves. *La vita è bella* (*Life is Beautiful*) (Roberto Benigni 1997 Italy) – made in Italy's Cinecittà – and *Astérix et Obélix contre César* (Claude Zidi 1999 France/Germany/Italy) – featuring effects work by France's post-production company Duboi – are successful examples of this new trend. In a special report on European inroads into special effects, Françoise Meaux Saint Marc (1999: 19) wrote:

Digital effects houses in the northern territories of France, Germany and the Benelux use some of the most advanced technology in the world. All are intent on securing more international business to underwrite the local television programming, commercials and feature productions that currently support the sectors.

She identified France as the location for high-end equipment but described the sector as 'spiralling out of control, with new companies opening every week, an over-investment in technology and lower profits' (p. 19).

Current moves towards animation and special effects production may not correspond to what is still regarded as national tastes, but do fulfil the expectations of young people – the biggest consumers of film today – for entertainment cinema. Along with action-packed thrillers, often made with US financing, animation and effects production reflects the growing trend for Europeans to make films for the international market. Whether this will help develop new local strengths is far from certain considering the high cost of technology and the inevitable arrival of greater competition.

Genres

European countries both attract and favour different genres. While most countries produce comedies and dramas, other genres (e.g. science fiction, thriller, animation) have proved less popular with European film-makers. The UK leads in romantic comedies and period dramas. Spain and Germany have a reputation for thrillers, even though France is rapidly catching up as a new generation of film-makers targets a teenage audience.

Comedies continue to be the most popular genre in their domestic markets, on both large and small screens. Rarely appreciated by film critics, comedies play an important part in sustaining the viability of many national industries. However, with the exception of UK and US titles (see Chapter 6), there is a widespread perception that foreign-language comedies do not travel well. Literary adaptations and historical costume dramas have served some industries well, but the cost of mounting such lavish productions has forced local producers to seek partners abroad. France, Ireland and the UK are among the most successful countries at producing large-scale historical films with high productions values including *Shakespeare in Love* (John Madden 1998 US), *Michael Collins* (Neil Jordan 1996 US), *Angela's Ashes* (Alan Parker 1999 US/UK) and *The General* (John Boorman 1998 Ireland/UK). There are many risks attached, however, to this type of production, as demonstrated by the poor theatrical performance during 1997 and 1998 of the co-productions *The Serpent's Kiss* (Philippe Rousselot 1997 France/Germany/UK) and *The Land*

Girls (David Leland 1998 UK/France). Other international co-productions with French input included *1492, Conquest of Paradise* (Ridley Scott 1992 UK/France/Spain), *La Reine Margot* (Patrice Chéreau 1994 France/Italy/Germany), *Le Hussard sur le toit* (*The Horseman on the Roof*) (Jean-Paul Rappeneau 1995 France) and *La Veuve de Saint-Pierre* (*The Widow of Saint-Pierre*) (Patrice Leconte 2000 France/Canada). Often these French costume dramas had main characters played by stars of national significance (Danan, 1996: 79): for example, Gérard Depardieu, Isabelle Adjani and Juliette Binoche, but also Catherine Deneuve in the films of Régis Wargnier, *Indochine* (1992 France) and *Est–Ouest* (1999 Bulgaria/France/Russia/Spain).

Evidence suggests that sales agents and distributors are guilty of a certain degree of conservatism in deciding which films to offer in the market. This has seen expectations arising over how certain genres become representative of particular national cinemas. British realism (e.g. the films of Ken Loach and Mike Leigh), British comedies and gangster films, Irish political thrillers or depictions of rural life, Italian comedies, Spanish black comedies, or France's auteur films, sell an image of these national industries abroad. As these impressions become accepted, so they reinforce and perpetuate particular types of domestic production.

Auteur Cinema

Since attempts at defining European cinema inevitably encompass auteur cinema, it seems appropriate to consider auteur film as a production trend, arguably, the European film genre par excellence. Developing from the intellectual climate of French film criticism in the 1950s, auteurism celebrates the centrality of the film director's vision. In Europe, this belief has had an enduring effect as directors continue to be either hailed as the greatest strength of European cinema or keeping European cinema stuck in a rut of artistic indulgence.

Complex debates about auteur-led or producer-driven projects continue to give rise to conflicts within the industry. Maurizio Nichetti, the Italian director of local successes such as *Ladri di Saponette* (*The Icicle Thief*) (1989 Italy) and *Volere Volare* (1991 Italy), bemoans the arrogance of film-makers in his country: in 1995 he lamented 'they are unaccustomed to thinking of cinema as an industry' and 'tend to make films just for themselves' (quoted in Dobson, 1995: 22). Often denounced in Britain (see Finney, 1996; Puttnam and Watson, 1997; Dale, 1997) as 'the French approach', celebration of the film director's – and sometimes the scriptwriter's – cultural status is widespread in Europe, particularly in smaller countries such as Belgium and Portugal, but also in Central and Eastern Europe. At an East–West seminar held in Vienna in 1992, the Polish director Krzystof Zanussi said that he could see only two options for cinema today: a cinema of directors (the European concept) and a cinema of producers (the Anglo-Saxon notion). For Zanussi, the latter reduced film production and distribution to a huge business enterprise, representing 'a nightmare' Europeans were to avoid at all costs.

However, drawing a distinction between an auteur-led and a producer-driven cinema is not as clear-cut as the advocates of the two approaches would have us believe. In the East, where there is a strong tradition of auteur cinema, the new business executives of the film industry are more compromising, preferring to reconcile artistic and commercial interests. A way in which artistic and economic interests become integrated is in how the artistry of the auteur is often used by distributors as one of the most marketable and profitable hooks for European films, as seen for example with the selling of a name like the Spanish director Pedro Almodóvar.

DEVELOPMENT AND TRAINING
Project Development
In Hollywood, film development consists of 'five major stages: idea generation, concept testing, product development, pre-launch market testing, and market introduction' (Hoskins *et al.*, 1997: 125–6). Compared to Hollywood, Europe still has no established tradition of script analysis or development. Martin Dale (1992) has described the process of story development as involving 'usually one-man teams with a few readers' and key decision criteria as often the result of 'personal choice rather than a detailed story or market analysis' (p. 39). In Europe, ideas of what is involved with development vary not only from one territory to another but also from one producer or project to another. Acknowledging these variations, the European Commission (1997) made clear that the

> development of a film project is crucial to its success, as its future prospects on the international markets are heavily dependent on it. Writing the screenplay, seeking partners, devising the production financing plan and planning the marketing and distribution are the preliminary stages in running a project that culminates in the beginning of production proper.

The Commission also commented:

> The number of projects at the development stage in comparison to the number in production is still very low in Europe, as is the level of investment at this stage in comparison with the total cost of a film. On average one film is produced per four

or five at the development stage in the EU, whereas in the United States the proportion is more like one to ten. And the portion of a film's budget devoted to development is only around 2% in Europe, as against 7%–10% in the United States.

Moves have been made that suggest that the film business in Europe seems to be slowly adopting a more strategic approach to development. Under the European Union's MEDIA programme, financial assistance to support development, distribution and training has been offered through successive phases (MEDIA I 1990–95, MEDIA II 1996–2000 and MEDIA Plus 2000–) (see Chapter 4). This has seen the launch of initiatives such as Support for Creative Independent Production Talent (SCRIPT), the MEDIA Business School seminars, and the Ateliers du Cinéma Européen (ACE), which played a major part in convincing many European producers that creative and financial planning for a project must proceed in tandem. Even though MEDIA consultants emphasise that 'the European industry also needs to remain true to itself in order to succeed' (Coopers & Lybrand, 1991: 8), they have repeatedly stressed that in Europe, too many films go into production compared to Hollywood where many projects never go further than the development stage and that, '[t]he best way to reinforce [the European film] industry – with all its inherent peculiarities – is to learn from other advanced industries such as the film industry in the US' (Labrada, 1995: 13).

Recognising the considerable costs involved and the heavy risks entailed by producers at the pre-production stage, national governments and European programmes like MEDIA have put forward incentives to encourage producers to invest adequately in an area 'traditionally regarded as secondary to the production process' (MEDIA II Programme). Aiming 'to share this risk with production companies by proposing reimbursable loans', in 1996 the MEDIA II Development Programme provided a financial package of 60 million ecus over five years. This development action line granted support to specific projects, production companies and 'industrial platforms' (e.g. CARTOON, see Chapter 4). The objectives of the programme were threefold:

- to encourage companies to plan project development as fully as possible
- to expand investment at that stage
- to abandon projects lacking real commercial prospects

Despite the MEDIA initiatives and increased transnational collaboration, development funds in Europe remain small and attitudes towards development continue to differ. Ireland and the UK have a conception of the development process closer to that of Hollywood. In France, Italy or Spain on the other hand, many film professionals disagree with MEDIA recommendations to adopt Hollywood methods as a normative framework. Research done in France and Italy (Dubet, 2000) shows that young aspiring directors who endorse a market-driven ideology belong to a minority there. Most see themselves as artists rather than creators of utilitarian products and think their creativity should be valued for its expressive qualities. Others (e.g. Vivancos, 2000) believe that editing – not pre-production – is the crucial stage for making a successful film. The influence of audience opinion on development is also different in Europe compared to Hollywood: according to a French agency specialising in test-screenings, tests are mainly used by clients who already have serious doubts about their films (Lafontaine, 1997). Nonetheless, national institutions (including the CNC in France and the Film Council in the UK) are putting more money into development funding, and today a new generation of producers is giving more importance to pre-production and script development.

CASE STUDY: *LOLA RENNT*

In the late 1990s, the German company X Filme Creative Pool GmbH was hailed as a paradigm of the new European cinema after producing the hit *Lola Rennt* (*Run Lola Run*) (1998).

Lola Rennt (*Run Lola Run*, 1998)

Directed by German film-maker Tom Tykwer, *Lola Rennt* was developed and produced by X Filme with the participation of Westdeutschen Rundfunk (West German Radio), ARTE, and with support from Filmstiftung Nordrhein-Westfalen, Filmförderung in Berlin-Brandenburg (the regional and promotion funds) and Bundesministerium des Innern (Germany's Ministry of the Interior).

Lola Rennt is a chase thriller about a young Berliner (played by Franka Potente) who only has a short time to find DM100,000 to save her boyfriend from his underworld crime boss. Lola runs her course three separate times to get it right. The film's makers were aiming to produce an entertaining but thoughtful thriller: '*Lola* is philosophical but you're not pushed into it. [...] You can enjoy it, but there's something to think about afterwards. This is the kind of movie that we should be producing – generating a new new wave,' claimed Tykwer on its US release (quoted in *Entertainment Weekly*, 1999: 39).

In an interview with Tykwer in 1999, Eric Rudolph (1999: 20) chronicled the origin of the film:

> *Lola* was born when Tykwer's imagination conjured up the image of a young
> woman sprinting across a major metropolis. Building on this notion, Tykwer drew
> further inspiration from his own 1992 short film *Because*, which was shot by Frank
> Griebe, who also photographed *Deadly Maria* and *Winter Sleepers* for the director.
> 'In *Because*, a couple argues and then starts up again, with the argument taking a
> different tack. [...] We had no money, so the entire film took place in their
> apartment. [On *Lola*] we thought we could set the idea outside and let it grow into
> something bigger and wilder. [...] We wanted [...] to organize time in a different
> way. To me, one of the miracles of film is that you can restructure time and do
> things you always wished you could do in reality but can't.'

Given the production's relatively limited resources – a budget of US$1.8 million (DM3.5 million) – the film had a tight twenty-eight-day schedule starting in April 1997. However, the pre-production process – including extensive storyboarding – took much longer. Tykwer has commented that time spent on development was time well spent: 'there [was] a need for discussions with all involved at the development stage [...] such discussions [turned] into a promotion effort'.[5] Even so, he deplored how in the current state of the industry, 'the promotion campaign is already in place before the movie is finished'.

Making an entertaining film does not exclude the notion of art. 'It is to make arty mainstream movies' that Tykwer, along with his producer Stefan Ardnt and directors Dani Levy and Wolfgang Becker, decided to form X Filme Creative Pool in the mid-1990s. Like many people of their generation, their tastes are eclectic. They 'admire Godard and like seeing many movies in one day: Wim Wenders' films and *The Matrix*, *American Pie* and *Dancer in the Dark*'.

To shoot his existential thriller, Tykwer used a variety of mixed media formats and techniques: video, 35 mm stock, animation, digital effects (produced by Werk AG), marking the passage of time with black-and-white photography for flashbacks and colour for flash-forwards. Faced with this bombardment of techniques, the view of US commentator Crissa-Jean Chappell (1999: 4) is understandable: 'Can we classify this mix of sound and image as a motion picture? Or is *Lola* a video-game? [...] a feature-length music video?' However, Tykwer is uneasy with the comparison of *Lola* to a video game. He insists that, with its three-act classic narrative structure, his film is closer to opera. *Lola Rennt* is layered with cinematic references to films as different as *Die Blechtrommel* (*The Tin Drum*) (Volker Schlöndorff 1979 West Germany/France) and *Sliding Doors* (Peter Howitt 1998 UK/US) and to the works of directors like Alain Resnais, Stanley Kubrick, Krzysztof Kieślowski and Quentin Tarantino. Winner of eight German awards, *Lola Rennt* was selected as the German entry for the best foreign-language film Oscar in 1998 and screened at various film festivals all over the world.

Lola Rennt illustrates the vitality of an emerging generation of European filmmakers who are prepared to give more importance to development and the pre-production phase than their predecessors. They are also at ease with the traditions of European auteur/art cinema and Hollywood entertainment values. The commercial potential of the X Filme team did not go unnoticed. In December 1998, the Berlin-based film collective signed an agreement with Miramax for X Filme to provide the speciality distributor with an exclusive first look at all properties owned, controlled or written by its members. In turn, Miramax submits projects to X Filme for its members to direct (Goodridge and Frater, 2000). Through this deal, Tykwer agreed to direct *Heaven* (2002 France/Germany/US), the first part of a trilogy planned by Kieślowski and writing partner Krzysztof Piesiewicz before the death of the Polish director in 1996. *Heaven* marked the English-language debut of Tykwer.[6] The director of *Lola Rennt* may claim that for him, 'film-making was never about going to Hollywood' and that he does 'not really care if [he does] a film in Germany, in America, in Japan or in Australia, if it fits a story' (quoted in Lewin, 1999: 71). Yet to many Europeans, Tykwer's *Heaven* is yet another example of how powerful Hollywood remains in both attracting European talent and taking over prestigious European projects.

Education and Training

Responsiveness to the changing world of film production means that training and re-training continues to be essential for participation in the industry. Training provides the film industry with 'a fertile breeding ground for creative and technical talent to develop' and 'has a direct effect on Europe's ability to consolidate on an existing skills base, and upon its creative and industrial growth potential' (Finney, 1996: 36).

Arguably training has a higher priority in the East than in the West. Graduates from prestigious schools such as FAMU, the famous Prague school, the University of Drama and Cinematography I. L. Caragiale of Bucharest, and Hungary's Béla Balázs Studio (BBS) have ended up working in local film and television studios. Short films by graduates regularly receive prizes at international film festivals. However, lack of funding impairs the ability of these schools to retain their status as centres of excellence as the rate of technical change and international competition intensifies.

The Hungarian situation is somewhat representative of that found in other countries of the former Eastern Bloc. Before political change, the Hungarian film industry was fed mostly by graduates from the College of Theatrical and Film Arts (including film directors, cameramen, producers and actors) who, after completing their studies, were practically guaranteed a job. In the post-Communist era, the number of students dropped considerably as employment routes dwindled, and today many graduates hope to move to the West. Before 1989, the main support for new talent in Hungary was the BBS where first films and experimental films were made. BBS now operates as a non-profit foundation and has lost most of its sponsorship.

In the West, formal education is provided by publicly supported film schools, along with university programmes involving practical production work, and a number of private schools. In the UK, the National Film and Television School and the Royal College of Art are the country's most prestigious schools. Germany has the Academy of Film and Television (Berlin), the Munich Film School and the Potsdam-Babelsberg Film School. Other significant schools are the National Film School of Denmark (Copenhagen), and the FEMIS and Ecole Lumière in France. Courses offered at these top institutions are oversubscribed and, as a result, these establishments tend to be very selective and are often labelled elitist. These schools have also changed their approach to teaching. 'Watching as many films as possible at the local *Cinémathèque*' (Claude Chabrol quoted in Frodon, 1995: 119) is no longer regarded as a reasonable approach to acquire film-making skills. All schools include courses on how to submit and complete a script and a business plan. They usually welcome foreign students and, under the aegis of the Centre International des Ecoles de Cinéma

(CILECT) and the Groupement Européen des Ecoles de Cinéma et Télévision (GEECT), encourage co-operation through exchanges and exhibitions of student work.

While universities and film schools in Western Europe offer basic acquisition and development of skills, informal on-the-job training has tended to predominate in the film industry, particularly for the technical crafts (Allen J. Scott, 2000a: 97). Unions and other professional associations protect the interests of their members in the freelance labour market, and have an active role to play in ensuring that workers entering the industry will continue to guarantee high professional standards.

New entrants to the film industry have usually found that short films or television commercials and documentaries offer a stepping stone to a career in feature films. Opportunities for the exhibition of short films have greatly increased over the last few years. The new digital television channels need short films to help fill their extensive schedules. Elsewhere, Internet companies are investing substantial venture capital into the sector. The Internet provides more exposure for short-film-makers and may, in the future, help them to get some money up-front (Kelly, 2000). In the theatrical sector, there has been a proliferation of short film festivals and many of the larger film festivals now often run a short film section. Some exhibitors have also started screening short films again to support their feature programmes.

Competition and technical changes have created a new demand for a properly skilled workforce, a factor acknowledged by increases in the training and development budget of the MEDIA programmes. Private sponsorship is also playing an increasing role in Europe.[7] Despite the fact that the share of the budget of the MEDIA programme devoted to training has regularly increased over the years, many in the film industry feel that the European Commission does not do enough to support Europe's film industries at a critical time. In December 2000, shortly after the announcement of the MEDIA Plus budget, the leader of France's trade association FICAM (Fédération des industries du cinéma, de l'audiovisuel et du multimédia) commented: 'They don't think the technical industries are part of the cultural industries. No national film production can exist without strong technical industries' (Caradec, 2000: 9). The FICAM has since pledged to lobby harder 'the technocrats in Brussels'.

PRODUCERS AND ENTREPRENEURS
The Importance of Producers
The roles and strategies adopted by producers vary greatly depending on the project, production company or national context. Many European producers remain insistent that their role is not simply to raise finance but is primarily

creative. Often in consultation with the director, the producer is responsible for assembling the screenplay, cast and crew. The producer also oversees the smooth running of the production during shooting, and ensures the delivery of the completed film to the distributor.[8] In the 1990s, emphasis was put on the producer's role in balancing film costs with potential receipts.

Noting how little continuity there was between development, production, marketing and exhibition in Europe, the MEDIA Business School set up a series of seminars to train producers, helping them to understand how to make well-financed pictures, and to face commercial realities. Producers received guidance on knowing how much to invest, making predictions about the film's market, evaluating the breadth of that market, the artistic scope of a film, and understanding the systems of subsidies and pre-sales. It was recommended that producers involve distributors and sales agents in making marketing decisions at the earliest stages of developing any concept.

In the countries of Central and Eastern Europe, before the 1990s, film units were usually led by well-established directors. They had a semi-autonomous status and functioned as basic film production entities. Producers were not the driving force behind projects. With funding coming centrally from state budgets, cast and crews did not need to know the exact cost of the productions on which they were working; their salaries were guaranteed (Iordanova, 1999a). During the 1990s, privatisation created a demand for film producers, and Western consultants were drafted in to provide training, information and networking opportunities for Eastern European producers. Training effectively had to start from scratch, but advancing the skills and business knowledge of producers was seen by many in the industry as a key priority for the region.

CASE STUDY: MARIN KARMITZ

Founder of MK2 Productions, Marin Karmitz is often regarded as the most powerful independent producer in France. His company is also one of the most aggressive distribution groups and exhibition chains in Paris. Karmitz prefers to describe himself as 'un éditeur et marchand de films', a publisher and dealer in films (Karmitz, 1994: 161): 'publisher' because of a passion 'to discover and to encourage others to discover new languages, unexplored territories' (ibid.);[9] 'dealer' because of his desire to cover all sectors of the supply chain to ensure that works of quality are made and exhibited, creativity is encouraged and pluralism maintained. MK2's reputation is built on producing work by high-profile French directors such as Claude Chabrol, Alain Resnais and Jean-Luc Godard. Karmitz has also produced films for major international directors, including the brothers Paolo and Vittorio Taviani (Italy), Ken Loach (UK), Alain Tanner (Switzerland), Theo Angelopoulos (Greece), Jiri Menzel (Czech Republic),

Lucian Pintilie (Romania), Pavel Lounguine (Russia) and Mohsen Makhmalbaf (Iran). In the early 1990s, his close relationship with Kieślowski resulted in MK2 co-producing the *Trois couleurs* trilogy.

Karmitz emerged in the French film world following the events of 1968. After directing *Camarades* (1970 France) and *Coup pour coup* (1972 France/West Germany), he was labelled a militant cinéaste. Becoming persona non grata with France's conservative film establishment, Karmitz realised that if a viable alternative to commercial cinema was to be maintained, another system of production, distribution and exhibition was needed. In order to preserve the identity of the films he liked, Karmitz embarked on creating his own cinema circuit. Acquiring his first theatre in 1973, the 14 Juillet–Bastille located in a popular area of Paris, Karmitz established a venue for screening foreign films in their original version. Since that time, taking risks has remained a constant in Karmitz's career. It is a strategy that has served him well. Today, Karmitz is at the head of a small empire. His company has a turnover of over €38 million and a 150-strong staff. His forty-four theatres in and around Paris include a thirteen-screen complex with catering facilities in the new development around the Bibliothèque Nationale de France in the XIIIth arrondissement.

However, Karmitz's rise to success was not always smooth. His associations with French conglomerates, Banque de Suez in the 1980s and Havas in 1996 (when a 20 per cent stake was sold to the French media group), were short-lived. MK2's distribution strength has been exploited and exported by former employees, benefiting from their previous experience, something Karmitz is said to resent (Frater, 1993). Karmitz's former employees include distributors Jean Labadie (founder of Bac Films), Fabienne Vonnier (founder of Pyramide), Francis Boespflug (who became chief programmer for the Gaumont circuit), and Alain Goldman, the producer of *1492, Conquest of Paradise*.

The former militant gauchiste turned businessman has been a member of numerous commissions and even advised Jack Lang, the French Minister of Culture, in the 1980s. A strong supporter of state intervention in the field of cinema – 'the only guarantee of freedom and dignity for individual artists' (quoted in *Forum du Conseil de l'Europe*, 1995: 34) – Karmitz is nevertheless very critical of governments in general and the French Socialists in particular. He accused the latter of wasting billions on cable and satellite while ignoring content and believes laissez-faire policy since 1985 has led to the arrival of a global distribution system which 'attacks the notion of content and imposes its own rules' (quoted in Frater, 1993). He strongly believes that 'in Europe, individuals should be able to express themselves, something which no longer exists in Hollywood or in the pale European imitations of the latter' (quoted in Simonnet, 1993: 43). In his autobiography, he writes:

The first rule is to ask yourself some questions: 'What kind of cinema are you fighting for, what are you trying to do?' [...] Nowadays, people sell the films before they make them. They sell them ... mainly to television companies. [...] And that means they want films that are 'safe', that have nothing to say. [...] They steer clear of anything that might upset people, anything new or off-centre – in other words, creative (Karmitz, 1994: 34).

As a producer, he has made some eighty films to-date. He sees his role as 'to accompany a film from its birth to its release' (*ibid.*). This also includes working on the poster, the trailer, choosing a release date, along with arranging international sales and festival screenings. He talks of 'the necessary harmony between the producer, the director and their team' (author's translation, quoted in Conter, 2000: 15). This implies 'talking about content first, not money' (*ibid.*). Karmitz admits that he is extremely demanding before and after the shooting of a film, but his background as a director has taught him to recognise the creative freedom of the director and he 'does not come and annoy the director on the set' (*ibid.*).

The man who accused broadcasters of investing only in films corresponding to what they believe are audiences' expectations, and the French conglomerates of monopolising France's screens, is not without paradoxes. He was, for a while, a shareholder of the French television channel M6 and many of his productions were co-produced by Canal Plus and ARTE – albeit with a much reduced television share than the average French production. Karmitz accused Gaumont and UGC of dumping practices but has now come under attack from French independent exhibitors who accuse him of resorting to the same unfair tactics as the larger circuits. In the summer of 2000, a few months after leading the campaign against UGC and its introduction of a controversial loyalty card (see Chapter 6), Karmitz joined Gaumont and launched 'Le Pass'. To justify his action, he said it was the only way 'to save his company and thirty years of work' (author's translation, Henochsberg, 2000).

As far as the producer's role is concerned, Karmitz's case raises important issues about creativity and independence, power and money, the necessity to expand, and about the possibility of choice but also the need to compromise.

Consolidating European Production

As the Karmitz case study illustrates, the distinction between independent and non-independent producers is becoming increasingly blurred. Arguably, the only independent producers are those who finance, out of their own resources, micro-budget and often provocative films which cannot find public or private investors. Predominantly made up of a large number of small production entities – some of which only work on a single film – Europe's production sector is in need of consolidation. Some territories (France, Belgium) introduced regulations to protect independent producers. Others used the American system as a model. In the UK, for instance, the principle of franchising was instigated to allocate funding from the National Lottery. Under this system, three awards were made for a period of six years. Each of the three successful bidders – the Film Consortium, Pathé Pictures and DNA films – were formed around very experienced producers.[10] MEDIA Plus also favours companies headed by experienced producers, with a number of on-going projects on their slate, and which can demonstrate solid relationships with financiers.

Behind the names of the auteurs of the 1960s were producers who wielded enormous power and worked in relative independence. Few producers today can, like Karmitz, claim to enjoy such advantages. Most of those who still do – Martin Dale (1997: 267–84) called them 'the Leading Contemporaries' – launched their career in the 1960s and usually work for or head a well-established company or a group. They include David Puttnam, Simon Relph and other producers from the Film Consortium in the UK. Other names are Dieter Geissler and Bernd Eichinger in Germany, Claude Berri in France, and Andres Vicente Gomez in Spain.

Following the enormous popular success of one or two of their films, a younger generation of producers rapidly acquired a similar status. Those who made their mark with major European releases in the 1990s include: Duncan Kenworthy, *Four Weddings and a Funeral* (Mike Newell 1994 UK); Andrew MacDonald, *Shallow Grave* (Danny Boyle 1994 UK) and *Trainspotting* (Danny Boyle 1996 UK); Alain Goldman, *1492, Conquest of Paradise*; Alain Rocca, *Un monde sans pitié* (*A World Without Pity*) (Eric Rochant 1989 France) and *La Discrète* (*The Discreet*) (Christian Vincent 1990 France); Fernando Bovaira, *La Lengua de las mariposas* (*Butterfly's Tongue*) (José Luis Cuerda 1999 Spain) and *Plenilunio* (*Plenilune*) (Imanol Uribe 2000 France/Spain); Domenico Procacci, *Il Partigiano Johnny* (*Johnny Partisan*) (Guido Chiesa 2000 Italy); and Stefan Ardnt, *Lola Rennt* (*Run Lola Run*) and *Absolute Giganten* (*Gigantic*) (Sebastian Schipper 1999 Germany). While many bemoan the lack of good producers in Europe, these names demonstrate how the region is continuing to produce talent with the necessary creative and business skills to compete in the international arena.

In the high-risk world of film-making, creative professionals frequently must turn into entrepreneurs. In Europe today, several directors and actors are tied to groups such as Bertelsmann in Germany, or Havas and the Seydoux Brothers in France (Dale, 1997: 160). Others have opted to set up their own production outfits in order to retain control over their work. The directors of some of Europe's most commercially successful films of the last two decades have become producers, for example Luc Besson, Mathieu Kassovitz, Pedro Almodóvar, Fernando Colomo, Nanni Moretti, Lars von Trier and Wim Wenders. They play a particularly important role in launching new talent able to capture the views and tastes of the younger public. Actors (e.g. Catherine Deneuve, Gérard Depardieu, Roberto Benigni) and other creative artists (e.g. the talented cinematographer Vlad Paunescu in Romania) have also joined the production bandwagon. Among the reasons they give for launching into production are the desire to retain creative control, and long-term professional and financial security.

In the East, many reputable directors are now heading film studios and/or companies, both public and privatised. In Romania for example, after the fall of Ceaucescu, Andrei Blaier, Mircea Daneliuc, Lucian Pintilie, Dinu Tanase and Sergiu Nicolaescu became the heads of production units previously operated by Romaniafilm, the state-owned film body. In Russia, Nikita Mikhalkov (*Utomly-onnye Solntsem* [*Burnt by the Sun*] [1994 France/Russia] and *Sibirskij Tsiryulnik* [*The Barber of Siberia*]) runs his own production company (TriTe).

CONCLUSION

In Europe's film industries, differences between working practices and philosophies continue to vary from one country to another. So do labour costs and technical facilities. Trends towards specialisation and de-localisation have greatly increased in the last ten years. Collaboration still largely occurs along national lines but is also rapidly moving towards European and even global configurations. As Europe's film industries face changing economic and technological conditions, investment in training seems ever more to be crucial. Alongside Europe's respected directors, the region's producing talent has played a vital role in sustaining the industry.

NOTES

1. The study was initiated by the Chambre Syndicale des Producteurs et Exportateurs de Films Français (CSPEFF), the Société Civile des Auteurs Réalisateurs Producteurs and the CNC. Entitled *Les Modes de Production Cinématographique en Europe*, the ARP study was financially supported by the CNC, PROCIREP, ARP and the CSPEFF.

2. As opposed to above-the-line costs (production costs relating to the creative elements including acquisition of rights and fees for the director, producer, writer and principal cast), below-the-line costs include production staff, camera, sound recording, art director, set construction, studio rent, wardrobe, make-up, props, film stock, laboratory charges and retakes (Dally, 1993).

3. Research done in Ireland by Coopers & Lybrand in the early 1990s showed that

every £1 million spent on film production created the equivalent of fifty full-time jobs a year (quoted in Duncan, 1995: 10).

4. For a more comprehensive survey of Eastern Europe's studios, see Iordanova (1999a).

5. Unless otherwise stated, all quotes from Tykwer are from the talk he gave at the Colloquium 'E la nave va ... pour un nouvel élan du cinéma européen' hosted by the European Film Academy and held at the Théatre de l'Odéon in Paris on 2 December 2000.

6. After *Lola*, Tykwer directed *Der Krieger und die Kaiserin* (*The Princess and the Warrior*) (2000 Germany) distributed outside North America and Germany by Le Studio Canal Plus. Initially a MK2 project, *Heaven* was subsequently developed by Noë Productions in Paris before the project was taken over by Miramax.

7. In the UK for instance, the Skills Investment Fund supports training schemes through voluntary contributions from film productions shooting in the country.

8. The term 'executive producer' is often used to refer to the person who accomplishes the latter activities but can also be used as a courtesy term for an executive of a company financing the film (Dally, 1995: 36).

9. All quotes from Karmitz, 1994, are translated from the French by the author.

10. Producers from the Film Consortium were: Sally Hibbins (Ken Loach's producer), Simon Relph (former director of British Screen with a good track record as a producer, he produced Louis Malle's film, *Damage* [1992 France/UK]), Anne Skinner, Nick Powell and Steve Woolley (from the then successful Palace Pictures, which ultimately went bankrupt).

3

Production Financing and Co-production

Film financing is undergoing major changes worldwide. There is no typical structure for financing film production in Europe, and there are many ways to raise finance. Investment levels vary significantly between territories (see table 3.1). Annual investment in film production within the European Union increased from US$1,132 million in 1988 to US$2,923.9 million in 1998, a 158.3 per cent growth in ten years. In 1998, France (32.9 per cent) and the UK (24.5 per cent) were by far the largest investors in film production in the European Union and made the highest average investments in films.

European productions remain predominantly low- and medium-budget films, in comparison to Hollywood films. Average film investments are low (US$4.26 million) in comparison with the average cost of a film from a major Hollywood

Table 3.1 European Film Production Investment (1988 and 1998)

	Production Investment			Average Investment per Film		
	1988	1998	98/88	1988	1998	98/88
	(US$m)	(US$m)	(%)	(US$m)	(US$m)	(%)
Austria		16.9			1.41	
Belgium	20.7	17.8	-14.0	1.38	2.54	+84.3
Denmark	13.9	39.0	+180.6	0.87	2.17	+149.4
Finland	4.6	18.1	+293.5	0.33	2.26	+588.6
France	415.9	963.4	+131.6	3.04	5.26	+73.4
Germany	96.1	342.5	+256.4	1.69	2.88	+70.7
Greece	7.2	7.4	+2.8	0.48	0.37	-22.9
Ireland	7.6	128.5	+1602.0	1.51	5.14	+240.4
Italy	269.7	361.6	+34.1	2.18	3.93	+80.7
Luxembourg	2.5	2.1	-16.0	2.50	0.70	-72.0
Netherlands	7.0	54.5	+648.6	0.39	3.03	+678.6
Portugal	5.8	4.5	-22.4	0.36	0.45	+24.1
Spain	79.5	206.4	+159.6	1.26	3.18	+151.6
Sweden		43.9			2.20	
UK	201.5	717.3	+256.0	5.04	8.24	+63.7
Total EU	1,132.0	2,923.9	+158.3	2.05	4.26	+107.2

Source: *Screen Digest* (1999b: 261)

studio (in 2000, US$76 million, US$51 million of which are direct production costs) (*Le Film français*, 2000b). However, following the growth of co-financing arrangements and the sharp rise of investment levels in some countries, a few European films can now claim a budget worthy of Hollywood. Figures given by the CNC show that annually, until 1987, only four French-initiated films a year had a production budget exceeding FF50 million. Ten years later, the figure for those films had risen to twenty-two a year. By 2001, eleven films had a budget over FF100 million. In 1999, *Astérix et Obélix contre César* was promoted as 'the most expensive film made in the French language'. Based on a famous comic strip that has been translated into seventy-seven languages, and claiming a FF270 million budget, the film was a French–German–Italian co-production with European stars (Gérard Depardieu and Roberto Benigni). Its sequel, *Astérix et Obélix: Mission Cléopâtre* (Alain Chabat 2002 France/Germany), had a FF327 million budget. In France, the highest-budgeted English-language productions have been Luc Besson's *The Fifth Element* (1997 France) (FF493.3 million, co-financed by Sony, Zalman and Gaumont) and *Joan of Arc* (FF360 million).

Regardless of the size of their budget, most European films are financed through a combination of public and private sources. This chapter is concerned with national sources of private and public finance, together with the financing of co-productions. Pan-European financing programmes are examined in the next chapter.

Joan of Arc (1999)

PRIVATE SOURCES OF FINANCING

Private financing for films is difficult to obtain because frequently investors are unprepared to take risks. Unlike in Hollywood, few producers in Europe have a steady slate of on-going projects capable of reassuring financiers. Very few producers are able to raise finance from a single source and most films entail a multiplicity of deals. A MEDIA Business School masterclass in film financing held in 1992 in Copenhagen, identified the following methods of raising finance from private sources:

- corporate finance (private investors, banks, completion guarantors)
- equity finance (finance institutions, broadcasters and other media groups)
- pre-sales (distribution rights)
- co-production finance
- sale of rights (television, video, etc.)
- other sources (sponsorship, product placement, sale of merchandising, licensing and publishing rights)

Deferrals (fees to producers, directors and artists payable only if a film proves financially successful) and facilities deals may also be added to this list.

Completion guarantors are organisations which, for a fee, guarantee funds to complete a film should the production go over budget (Petrie, 1991: 74). In the UK, where the practice is more common than in the rest of Europe, the completion guarantor's fee has been estimated at 6 per cent of the direct budgeted cost of a film (*Eyepiece*, 1987: 70). Equity investors expect to recover their investment plus interest and to have a share of the eventual profits of the film. Pre-sales are the funds raised by a producer (or a sales agent) for the financing of a film before it is completed and often consist of obtaining a minimum guarantee for distribution rights in a foreign territory. Pre-sales take the form of either a cash advance against distribution rights for the finished film or a distribution guarantee which can be discounted by a bank providing funds in the form of a loan to a film-maker. With a European film, an unaffiliated distributor will normally insist upon an all-media (cinema, television, video) distribution agreement in order to guard against the risks of theatrical exhibition (Thomas, 1996: 508).

Financial Institutions

A widening of the range of outlets for films (cable, satellite, pay-per-view), together with the development in recent years of more potentially commercial projects by European film-makers, has seen banks expressing increased interest in financing film production. While Italy's Banca Nazionale del Lavoro is probably the longest active financial institution in the field, several other European banks have now developed credit facilities for film production. They include CIC, Crédit du Nord, OBC and Worms in France, several banks associated with the Länder (e.g. Bavaria and Berlin) in Germany, Caja de Madrid and Banco Exterior (BEX) in Spain, ING in the Netherlands, BIL in Luxembourg, and Barclays and Guinness Mahon in the UK. However, banks are not in the business of taking risks: they ensure their loans are secured against pre-sales to credit-worthy distributors and rarely lend to producers without a completion guarantee. This has resulted in a situation where few banks have granted loans to production companies unless they were well-established groups, with substantial assets in the form of holding rights to large catalogues of audiovisual content.

Insurance companies have also started to show interest in film finance. Many productions face a financing gap between the value of contractual payments and the negative cost, that is, the total monies spent on the production of a film up to the point where the negative can be delivered to a principal distributor. Some insurance companies have provided cover on gap financing in the major European territories.

Guarantee Fund Proposals

A stable financial structure is a necessary condition for the maintenance of a steady output of films. To this end, film-makers have lobbied the European Commission (EC) to establish a venture capital scheme specifically for financing film projects. At the EC's conference on Film and Television in June 1994, a proposal was put forward for setting up a special fund raised through contributions from financial institutions to cover risks inherent in the film business. Aiming to benefit the production sector directly by helping to increase the funding available to European films with international appeal and profit-making potential, the European Guarantee Fund (EGF) was subsequently set up and allocated 90 million ecus in November 1995.[1] Adopted by the European Parliament, the proposal encountered strong opposition from Germany and the UK, and was unable to achieve unanimous agreement in the European Council.

Other proposals followed, notably under the Irish (1996) and Portuguese (1997) presidencies. At the end of the French presidency in 2000, it was announced that the Luxembourg-based European Investment Bank (EIB) would become involved with funding 'content' projects over the course of the next few years as part of the Innovation 2000 Initiative (i2i). The plan covered the whole information sector and included loans to finance infrastructure projects, together with research and training projects. The new strategy of co-operation was announced on 19 December 2000 in a joint press release:

The European Commission, the European Investment Bank (EIB) and the European Investment Fund (EIF) are proposing a new strand of activity to the European audiovisual industry so as to reinforce its financial basis and to accelerate its adaptation to digital technologies. Supplementing the MEDIA Plus programme (2000–2005), the purpose of this financial package is to improve the industry's competitiveness and to promote the development of European audiovisual content (EC Documents, 2000).

Along with EIF participation aimed at encouraging 'the emergence of an effective risk capital market', three other action lines were presented:

- provision by the EIB of credit lines (or 'global loans') to the banking sector specialising in the audiovisual media for funding small firms working in the field of audiovisual creation and technology and firms doing subcontracting work in this sector
- medium- and long-term financing by the EIB in co-operation with the banking sector, of large public and private television groups and of audiovisual production and distribution groups for their infrastructure (studios, digital installations, broadcasting stations, etc.) and creative work (production of 'bouquets' of films, distribution of works or catalogues)
- actions by the EIB and the European Commission designed to ensure better complementarity between banking resources and the Community subsidies under the MEDIA Plus programme

This plan was welcomed by the European Film Companies Alliance (EFCA) whose members include Studio Canal Plus and Pathé in France, the UK's Film-Four, and Portugal's Lusomundo Audiovisuais. Whether it will prove more successful than previous attempts at reinforcing the financial basis of the European film industry remains to be seen.

PUBLIC SOURCES OF FINANCING

The diversity of private sources for funding film production is matched by a whole array of measures taken by European governments over the years to support their national film industries. In both the East and the West, government support in the form of automatic and selective aids, tax breaks (including VAT exemption) and soft loans, continues to be instrumental as the first cornerstone of film financing. In the past, governments have favoured an approach based on selective funding for projects rather than companies. This approach may have suited film production activity in the 1960s and 70s but, as arguments for the development of a strong economic sector intensified, new investment incentives and funding mechanisms for production companies have been introduced. These have greatly contributed to encourage private investment in the film industry.

Forms of Government Support to Production

National and/or local governments support film for a variety of economic and cultural reasons. In the smaller territories, such as Denmark, Belgium and the Netherlands, the very existence of a film industry is largely dependent on government regulation and subsidies. Among the 'positive' forms of government support provided to the film industries of Europe, consultancy firm Coopers & Lybrand identify the following:

- direct investment in production through either outright grants, soft loans, credits or guarantees
- lines of credit, underwriting or advances secured against potential box-office receipts
- tax concessions on production costs or investment, or on revenue from exploitation
- premiums on currency exchange rates
- preferential treatment for indigenous productions on cinema release by financial support measures (e.g. tax or levy rebates to exhibitors for showing local films, or cash bonuses related to box-office performance)
- help in kind for provision of (subsidised) production facilities and other practical support (location finding and managing, logistics, state-owned studios, transport, soldiery as extras, etc.)
- awards or premiums for productions judged to be of value to national culture or which have been successful in international film festivals (Coopers & Lybrand, 1991: 12)

Contributions from government have tended to account for the majority of public funding in Europe, but taxes on cinema tickets, or television and video distribution, along with contributions from television companies, have also counted.

Martin Dale (1997) is representative of those critics who accuse European producers of a 'subsidy trap' mentality, spending most of their time chasing public funds: 'They are dependent on the state and secure funding through connections and lobbying' (p. 225). European producers may occasionally complain that state funding is over-bureaucratic and, in some cases, biased and/or elitist, but few could do without it.

In Central and Eastern Europe, state funding has been replaced by public funding bodies that still grant subsidies on a project basis. Traditionally, the

Table 3.2 Film Production (Co-productions) in EU Member States (1989–2000)

	1989	1990	1991	1992	1993	1994	1995	1996	1997	1998	1999	2000
Austria		14 (5)	11 (0)	14 (0)	26	24	19 (2)	15 (2)	15 (3)	22 (5)	20 (5)	24 (3)
Belgium	10	12 (9)	3 (3)	13 (8)	10 (4)	15 (6)	10 (8)	12 (6)	8 (5)	7 (6)	14 (5)	9 (8)
Denmark	18 (2)	13 (1)	11 (6)	15 (5)	14 (3)	17 (3)	17 (4)	21 (8)	23 (7)	18 (12)	16 (6)	24 (7)
Finland	10	13 (3)	12 (6)	10 (8)	13 (2)	11 (4)	8 (4)	11 (2)	10 (1)	8 (1)	16 (1)	11 (4)
France*	136 (70)	146 (65)	156 (83)	155 (83)	152 (85)	115 (54)	141 (78)	134 (60)	163 (77)	183 (81)	181 (66)	171 (60)
Germany [1]	68 (15)	48 (10)	72 (19)	63 (10)	67 (17)	60 (11)	63 (26)	64 (22)	61 (14)	50 (11)	74 (30)	90 (n/a)
Greece	8	13	15	15 (3)	16 (3)	12	19 (17)	17 (10)	16 (10)	15	16	20 (7)
Ireland	3	3	1	4	17 (2)	17	22	18 (12)	22 (6)	25	23	22 (7)
Italy	117	119 (21)	129 (18)	127 (13)	106 (20)	95 (24)	75 (15)	99 (22)	87 (16)	92 (13)	108 (16)	103 (17)
Luxembourg	3	1	2 (1)	4 (2)	2 (2)	0	0	5 (5)	5 (5)	3 (3)	2 (2)	3 (3)
Netherlands	13	13	14	13 (0)	16	16 (4)	18 (8)	18 (6)	15 (6)	18 (5)	14 (8)	25 (n/a)
Portugal	7	9 (7)	9 (3)	8 (7)	16 (8)	13 (9)	12 (11)	8 (6)	13 (4)	10	10	12 (5)
Spain	47 (8)	47 (10)	64 (18)	52 (14)	56 (15)	44 (8)	59 (22)	91 (25)	78 (25)	67 (20)	97	98 (34)
Sweden	26	25 (5)	27 (17)	20 (11)	29 (8)	23 (8)	23 (13)	18 (15)	29 (4)	20 (7)	23 (10)	n/a (11)
UK**	30	60 (8)	59 (22)	47 (13)	67 (29)	84 (32)	78 (36)	128 (52)	116 (51)	88 (45)	103 (26)	90 (43)

Sources: *CNC Info* (2001b); **Dyja (1999); EAO (2001a); *Screen Digest* (1997 and 2001b); and Thomas (1995)

Note:
1. From 1991 are figures for the reunited Germany.

budgets that financed the public funding agencies came mainly from receipts or a tax on admissions. As a result of an alarming decline in cinema attendance in the 1990s, most boards and commissions have very limited funds at their disposal. The funds they award may represent between 10 and 50 per cent of the estimated budget, and it can take years to raise financing for a film. For example, the director Alexei German took seven years to find funding for his 1998 Cannes competition film, *Khroustaliov, ma voiture!* (*Khroustaliov, My Car!*) (1998 France/Russia). Moreover, as Dina Iordanova (1999a: 49) points out:

> High inflation rate further affects the nominal value of the grant which often ends up covering a lower percentage of the production costs than initially estimated. Who receives funding and who gets the chance to work is an important issue, and it cannot be denied that there are instances of preferential treatment. Fights over alleged unfairness in funding awards re-emerge in the media of Eastern Europe nearly every year.

Poland has experienced a significant rise in film production in recent years (thirty-five films in 2000). The increased popularity of locally produced films (up to 40 per cent of the Polish theatrical market) has encouraged local distributors to become involved in financing domestic films (*Screen Digest*, 2001b: 378).

When analysing Europe's film industries in 1991, Coopers & Lybrand noted enormous disparities in production levels between countries, and suggested that these differences were not necessarily correlated with levels of government support. Since then, the range and scope of government-led initiatives to encourage investment have increased across Western Europe. Almost a decade after the Coopers & Lybrand report, in those countries where government has introduced new support mechanisms and incentives (Denmark, Luxembourg and Austria after 1992, Italy after 1998, Ireland since 1993, Spain and the UK since 1996), production levels have risen substantially (see table 3.2).

France's Incentives for Film and Television in the 1980s

France has the most comprehensive support system in Europe and, in the 1980s, the French socialist government was at the forefront of initiatives for fostering credit and investment in the audiovisual industries. At the instigation of the French Ministry of Culture, the Institut pour le Financement du Cinéma et des Industries Culturelles (IFCIC) was created in 1983 to provide, by means of a guarantee fund with mixed capital, a wide range of financial measures including credit for film production and completion guarantees for international productions. IFCIC support enabled financial institutions to protect their risks with guarantees of usually between half and two-thirds of the credit extended.

Table 3.3 Financing Sources for French-initiated Films (1990–2000)
(%)

	French Producers	SOFICAs	Automatic Aid	Selective Aid	Television		Distributors France	Foreign Input
					Co-prod.	Pre-buy		
1990	42.4	6.7	7.6	5.4	3.9	15.9	2.8	15.3
1991	33.7	5.9	7.6	4.7	4.6	18.9	4.4	20.2
1992	36.5	6.1	5.8	4.6	5.4	24.7	5.4	11.5
1993	33.4	5.2	7.7	5.5	5.6	25.2	5.1	12.3
1994	29.3	5.3	7.5	6.7	6.5	27.4	5.0	12.3
1995	26.8	5.6	8.7	5.7	6.8	30.1	4.0	12.3
1996	24.3	4.8	8.3	4.9	7.7	34.3	5.5	10.2
1997	33.4	4.5	7.7	5.2	7.2	28.7	3.5	9.8
1998	27.9	4.3	7.8	4.4	7.0	31.5	6.8	10.3
1999	28.0	4.4	6.8	4.4	6.0	34.2	8.8	7.5
2000	31.9	5.7	6.6	3.6	9.0	31.2	5.5	6.5

Source: *CNC Info* (2001b)

In 1996, the IFCIC provided loan guarantees for fifty-three films out of the 134 films produced in France (Bizern and Autissier, 1998: 95). Other countries followed suit, including Belgium, Spain, Switzerland and, in 1998, Italy.

In 1985, France adopted a new tax shelter scheme, the Sociétés de Financement de l'Industrie Cinématographique et Audiovisuelle (the SOFICAs), designed to introduce private funds into film production. Operated by a group of professional interests such as banks, production and distribution companies, the SOFICAs were highly regulated, only financing productions that had received CNC approval or were made by French producers. Under the scheme, it was required that a minimum 35 per cent of funds raised be allocated to independent producers. Investors could not, however, invest their money directly into a specific production. Investors bought shares in SOFICAs with the requirement that those shares be retained for a minimum of five years. Managers of each SOFICA decided which projects to finance on behalf of investors. Shareholders in SOFICAs were granted tax relief on the sums they invested. To encourage investment, the French government stipulated individuals could place up to 25 per cent of their taxable income into the SOFICAs tax free. Companies could benefit from a tax write-off of 50 per cent of total investment. Critics of the system today say that because SOFICAs are private funds whose aim is to create a profit for their shareholders, they take few risks with projects and prefer to invest in large-budget productions with well-known stars. Returns for investors have been limited and the scheme has subsequently been modified to attract more corporate investment.

In France, contributions to film financing by producers and the SOFICAs declined in the first half of the 1990s, before showing a slight increase to remain relatively stable in the second half of the decade (see table 3.3). At the same time, increased investment was made by distributors and particularly by television companies. This explains why the overall share of the SOFICAs' contributions to the financing of French-initiated films declined from 6.7 per cent in 1990 to 4.3 per cent in 1998 (4.4 per cent in 1999). In 2000, the creation of two new SOFICAs raised the proportion of funding from this source.

Until now, schemes such as the IFCIC and the SOFICAs have operated only at a national level. In early 2001, at a meeting of the recently funded Academy of Franco-German Cinema, film professionals announced their intention to create a Franco-German SOFICA. This would certainly represent a first step towards European harmonisation. It would also entail a major overhaul of the two countries' support systems.

Automatic and Selective Aids

Belgium, Finland, France, Germany, Italy, Portugal, Spain and Sweden operate automatic aid mechanisms for film production that work along similar lines.[2] In each case, the government raises money by imposing a levy on the sale of all cinema tickets, regardless of the nationality of the films concerned. Some or all of this money is then redistributed to domestic producers, with the level of payment determined by the number of admissions (and/or level of television earnings) achieved by their films. Under the French and Belgian systems, automatic aid is available in the form of credits to local producers on the condition that it is reinvested in the production of new films. This can also be used to pay secured debts (e.g. deferrals). There are other variations: in Spain, automatic aid is based on a film's budget, whereas in Germany and Austria, certain quality criteria apply (Schmitt, 1992).

All European countries offer some form of selective aid for film. The balance between selective and automatic aid varies between countries, however in most cases selective aid accounts for the highest proportion of funding available (see table 3.4). Selective aids, such as the French 'advance on receipts', usually go to projects which, arguably, could not be financed without public funding, that is, first films and works with cultural ambitions. In theory, the loan is repayable. In practice, only around 10 per cent of films are successful enough at the box office to repay the loan. Projects are assessed by committees. In France and Belgium, the aid takes various forms corresponding to the different stages in the production of a film. Denmark operates two support schemes, one aimed at films for mainstream adult audiences, the other at children's films. Selective aids administered by the Greek Film Centre are reserved for films of artistic merit, and prize-winning films

Table 3.4 Balance Between Selective and Automatic Support for Production

	Selective Support (Ecu millions)	Selective Support (%)	Automatic Support (Ecu millions)	Automatic Support (%)
Belgium	9.56	72	3.79	28
Denmark*	14.71	83	2.92	17
Finland*	7.53	100		
France*	54.92	29	131.37	71
Germany*	66.23	90	7.26	10
Greece	4.71	100		
Iceland	0.60	100		
Ireland*	3.75	100		
Italy*	84.03	92	7.31	8
Luxembourg	1.03	100		
Netherlands	28.95	100		
Norway [1]	7.55	68	3.58	32
Portugal*	3.91	68	1.81	32
Spain*	11.15	52	10.38	48
Sweden	11.40	75	3.80	25
Switzerland	8.07	100		
UK [2]	11.34	100		

Source: Bizern and Autissier (1998).
* 1995 figures

Notes:
1. For 1995, it is also necessary to add the support given by the Foundation for Audiovisual Production (figures not provided).
2. For 1995, it is also necessary to add 16.74 million ecus of National Lottery support to 'Selective Support' total.

benefit from subsidies provided by the Cinematographic Affairs Directorate of the Ministry of Culture. The Portuguese Film Institute allocates financial aid for scriptwriting, development and production by means of examination.

In the 1990s, several countries witnessed a shake-up in their funding structures under reforms initiated by European and international legislation. These measures tended to encourage producers to make more commercial films via conditionally repayable loans (Austria), automatic subsidy schemes based on the performance of a film at the box office (Spain since 1995), revised automatic aid (France), or tax breaks (Iceland, Ireland, Luxembourg, the Netherlands and the UK).

Support schemes in many European countries are not restricted to domestic productions. Some, for example the Vienna Film Financing Fund, or several German regional funds, have granted easy conditions of access to foreign productions. A trade report on 'Germany in the new millennium' stated that, in the late 1990s, 'a rash of private film funds raised literally billions of marks from private German individuals wanting to reduce their tax burden by investing in productions around the globe' (Barraclough, 2000). Naturally, non-German producers, notably the US studios, were quick to tap into these funds.

Compared to other countries seeking to attract overseas – especially American – productions, France has mainly promoted investment growth within the domestic sector but has also developed limited schemes to encourage co-productions with foreign partners (see below).

CASE STUDY: TAX BREAKS IN IRELAND, ICELAND AND LUXEMBOURG

In Ireland, the introduction of tax breaks has been seen as the financial base of a national cinema and the key to the success of establishing an Irish audiovisual industry (Barton, 2001). Set up in 1987, Section 35 of the Finance Act allowed companies to claim tax relief on sums up to IR£100,000 invested in qualifying films. Subsequent amendments included raising the amounts of money involved, making the scheme more attractive to corporate investors while opening it to individuals (1993), encouraging investment in off-peak production (1995), and incentives to encourage producers to locate their post-production work in the country (1997). Following these changes, the scheme was overhauled and renamed Section 481.

To qualify for Section 481 funding, films were required to meet the following conditions:

- be shot in Ireland and create employment there
- contribute returns to the Exchequer
- enhance Irish culture

As Barton (2001) notes, the last condition remained 'a rather vague concept in official documents'. Investments had to be made for a minimum of three years and investors had little say in the final product. With other territories, particularly those close to home such as the Isle of Man or the UK, also introducing tax breaks, the Irish scheme lost some of its attraction to overseas companies. Speaking at a European Cinema Conference held in Bangor, Ruth Barton (2001: 4) commented:

These incentives have been aimed at encouraging foreign productions to shoot in Ireland (with knock-on benefits in terms of training and services) and local filmmakers to raise investment money. However, the increase in European and international incentives for overseas film-making has lowered Ireland's competitiveness in this respect and, currently, the relative weakness of the Irish pound against sterling and the US dollar is largely responsible for maintaining the inflow of overseas productions. The attractiveness of the scheme has also been lessened by the fall in Irish taxation rates.

Critics of Section 481 condemn the scheme for its lack of transparency, the bureaucracy involved, and the cost of putting packages together. They also believe that the cost to the Exchequer is too high. Despite the criticisms, in 1999, a strategic report on planning the development of the Irish film and television industry argued for the retention and expansion of Section 481 (Film Industry Strategic Review Group, 1999).

Iceland has a disproportionately active industry for such a small country. The industry has benefited from the introduction of a tax refund scale according to the level of investments made by local companies and individuals in productions shot in the country. Also aimed at attracting foreign producers, the scheme has no Icelandic language or cast requirement (Söderbergh Widding, 1998).

In Luxembourg (population 400,000), producers are eager to stress their system of investment incentives is 'a fiscal mechanism, not a tax break' (anonymous interview source). Under the Certificat d'Investissement Audiovisuel (CIAV) – first introduced in 1988, amended in 1993, and renewed in 1998 for a period of ten years – any company financing a production can recoup a proportion of qualifying production costs in the form of tax certificates, if those costs are demonstrably incurred during production in Luxembourg. Under Luxembourg's former tax relief arrangement, there was no requirement for the producer to be a native or a resident of the country as long as a large part of the film's budget was spent in Luxembourg. Until the late 1990s, the CIAV scheme was automatic, but it now operates selectively, with the government issuing certificates only to companies that have received the formal agreement of the National Audiovisual Production Fund. Today, production activity in Luxembourg is at its highest since the introduction of the scheme.

The importance of tax breaks for the building or survival of a film industry must not be overestimated. In the Netherlands, tax incentives were introduced in 1997. However, the Dutch Federation of Film Interests has argued the system benefits mainly foreign producers and does not contribute to building up the domestic industry infrastructure (*Screen Digest*, 2000b). This criticism may also be relevant to other territories.

Competition and Harmonisation

In Europe as a whole, the introduction of new measures to stimulate investment in film production has created more competition between territories for foreign investments. In the late 1990s, the German region of North Rhine Wesphalia (NRW) was so successful in luring projects away from the Netherlands with its subsidies that Dutch film companies complained to the European Commission. Interestingly, the trend in Western Europe as a whole is now to adopt a system similar to the NRW scheme – designed to assist the producer in maintaining an on-going business rather than supporting individual projects – and/or to move towards a system modelled on the French SOFICAs.

Across Europe, the conditions defining funding schemes have tended to be bounded by national frameworks of thinking, looking inwards towards supporting domestic productions. As *Screen Digest* (1999b: 261–2) notes, since each territory continues to 'guard their incentive mechanisms jealously, [only] opening up in the case of co-productions', harmonisation of incentives across Europe still seems a long way away.

However, there are signs that some schemes are prepared to open out their funds to the wider regional economy and move towards greater 'Europeanisation'. For example, the French system – the most sophisticated funding system in Europe and reputed to be one of the most difficult to access for non-indigenous producers – was recently revised to allow, through a complex point system, European productions (totalling twenty-five points) to access its production support fund. However, this is still a far cry from the suggestion made in 1996 by the European Producers Club to adopt a proposal allowing producers based in countries operating automatic support systems to access each other's schemes as long as the films made could be defined as European (through a points system similar to the Council of Europe's Eurimages scheme).[3]

TELEVISION FINANCING

Broadcasters are now the most important sources of film financing in Europe. In several countries broadcasters are, by law, obliged to make direct contributions to the budgets of existing film funds. Broadcasters' investment in film varies between countries and companies, and can take three forms: co-production, pre-sales or acquisition of rights (usually for one or two screenings after a film's theatrical release). The value of the latter is normally determined by the box-office success of the film.

In France, broadcasters are encouraged to invest because co-producer status allows them to show films earlier. Since 1990, the country's five terrestrial television channels have been required to invest at least 3 per cent of their turnover in film production. In order to ensure the independence of producers from broadcasters, the channels could co-produce only through a subsidiary dedicated to such activities, and their contribution could not exceed 50 per cent of the film budget or of the French share of the budget. Pay-TV company Canal Plus has made the largest investment in film production in the country.[4] A separate feature-film law applies to Canal Plus, which invests around 20 per cent of its turnover in film acquisition. Since 1993, 60 per cent of the amount Canal Plus spent on acquiring rights was dedicated to European works, 45 per cent of which went to French-language films.

In France, all broadcasters invest in first feature films as well as large-budget pictures. Differences between channel identities evident in the mid-1990s (Jäckel, 1999: 182) seem less apparent today. However, it has been the case that private broadcasters have preferred to make substantial investments in the most expensive productions. For example, TF1 contributed FF22 million to the FF200 million budget of the Gérard Depardieu vehicle, *Vatel* (Roland Joffé 2000 France/US), and FF33 million went to the FF113 million budget of *Le Prince du Pacifique* (Alain Corneau 2000 France/Spain). However, ten out of the twenty-one films in which the private channel invested were directed by first-time film-makers.

Public and private (including cable) broadcasters in Belgium also contribute to film financing, and in the Netherlands, television channels must contribute to film financing through a complex system via a co-production fund. The Swiss public service channel also has an agreement with the film industry that sets the level of support to be granted by the channel to film producers in the form of co-productions. Since 1999, Spanish broadcasters are obliged to invest 5 per cent of their turnover in European film and audiovisual production, and new operators Via Digital and Canal Satellite have also begun investing in film. In Germany, the television companies ZDF and ADR contribute to the budget of the Filmförderungsanstalt (FFA), the main public funding agency. Compared to France, contributions by broadcasters (DM18.8 million in 1997) are far less important in Germany. However, government subsidies usually go to films that already have television backing.

Italian public broadcaster RAI is required to invest a proportion of its revenue in film production, and in 2000, created its film arm, RAI Cinema, to handle production and international sales (*Screen Digest*, 2000a). After Silvio Berlusconi's Fininvest spent huge sums of money on the acquisition of American films, it was decided in 1994 that pay-television channels should devote 10 per cent of their annual profits to national film production. It has been estimated that Italian broadcasters contribute 40 per cent of the total film production financing in the country (Dubet, 2000: 227).

In the UK, broadcasters are under no obligation to invest in film production, but Channel 4 has a long tradition of commissioning films since the broadcaster started operating in 1982. During the 1990s, the BBC and independent television channels started to follow suit. In 1999, twenty-five films by UK producers received backing from domestic and foreign television companies. FilmFour and BBC Films were the most active with, respectively, investments of £44 million in ten films and £21.32 million in seven films. In the Irish Republic, the public service broadcaster RTÉ funds feature film-making through equity investment or the purchase of transmission rights. However, in recent years:

[RTÉ] has come under criticism from the film-making community for its lack of commitment to Irish feature film-making. In its defence, it has claimed that the cost per hour of feature films is often considerably higher than that of a top-of-the-range television drama series – and the latter gain higher ratings (Barton, 2001: 5).

These tensions and concerns are also shared by other European countries.

Among European broadcasters, the Franco-German cultural channel ARTE stands out, both for its support of a cultural cinema and its investments in European co-productions. The channel invests most of its small budget in Europe-wide productions.[5] Since its launch in 1990, ARTE has been involved in acquiring, commissioning and co-producing well over 200 films. They include films directed by film-makers of almost every nationality in Europe. Many are co-productions between various European countries and include Theo Angelopoulos' *To Vlemma tou Odyssea* (*Ulysses' Gaze*) (1995 Greece/France/Italy/Germany/UK), Alain Berliner's *Ma vie en rose* (1997 France/Belgium/UK/Switerland), Peter Greenaway's *The Baby of Mâcon* (1993 UK/France/Germany/Netherlands), Alexei German's *Khroustaliov, ma voiture!*, Aki Kaurismäki's *Leningrad Cowboys Meet Moses* (1994 Finland/France/Germany), Ademir Kenovic's *Savrseni Krug* (*Perfect Circle*) (1997 Bosnia-Herzegovina/France/Netherlands), Michael Haneke's *Die Klavierspielerin* (*The Piano Teacher*) (2001 Austria/France/Germany), Lucian Pintilie's *Un été inoubliable* (*An Unforgettable Summer*) (1994 Romania/France) and *Trop tard* (*Too Late*) (1996 France/Romania), and Lars von Trier's *Breaking the Waves* (1996 Denmark/Sweden/France/Netherlands/Italy) and *Dancer in the Dark* (2000 Denmark/Germany/Netherlands/US/UK/France/Sweden/Italy/Finland/ Iceland/Norway).

In Central and Eastern Europe, television has also become an important source of funding for feature films. Local features are considered particularly attractive for prime-time programming slots, and broadcasters have been eager to invest in order to guarantee future broadcasting rights (Iordanova, 1999a: 50). Most territories have introduced regulations for broadcasters to invest in local films. In Poland, for instance, the two state-run channels are involved in production activities, and most Czech and Slovak films are receiving some form of funding from television (p. 50). However, in countries struggling through deep economic crises (e.g. Bulgaria and Romania), investing in cultural production and the enforcement of cultural legislation has not been a priority.

European companies investing in the new pay-television channels have become powerful players (e.g. Canal Plus in France, BSkyB in the UK, Nethold [now merged with Canal Plus] and Kirch in Germany) and show a keen interest in film production. They have joined forces with existing production outfits and/or launched their own production division, for example Canal Plus' Studio

Dancer in the Dark (2000)

Canal. Several broadcasters now invest in the films of other European countries. Germany's WDR and CLT-Ufa, and France's TF1 and Canal Plus, all invested in British films in the late 1990s.

With or without government legislation and/or incentives, broadcasters and media groups have now become major investors in Europe's film industries. However, there is some evidence to suggest that broadcasters are losing some of their interest in film. A recent report published by France's regulatory body, the Conseil Supérieur de l'Audiovisuel (CSA), shows that French broadcasters now rarely screen French contemporary films in prime time. Referring to the CSA report, *Cahiers du cinéma*'s Elisabeth Lequeret (2000a) infers that broadcasters are becoming less interested in film production, preferring instead to invest in sports, television series and talk shows. She suggests that, increasingly, only the pay-television channels take a positive view of cinema as an important showcase for the films they help finance.

CO-PRODUCTION AND CO-FINANCING

As noted earlier, few films produced in Europe today are financed solely by one production company. Most are co-productions. Co-production is a much abused term: it may refer to any form of co-financing (a pre-sale to a television channel, theatrical distributor or foreign territory) or creative and financial collaboration between various producers (including broadcasters). In recent years, co-financing arrangements have been more popular than the cumbersome inter-governmental co-production agreements.

All governments in Europe have bilateral and/or multilateral co-production agreements under the terms of which technical and artistic contributions must match the financial input.[6] At the instigation of the Council of Europe, these agreements were supplemented by the European Convention on Cinematographic Co-production in October 1992. It was the intention to use the Convention in order to simplify existing tripartite co-production agreements and the old – often deemed inflexible – bilateral treaties.[7] Under the Convention, the term 'European cinematographic work' referred to those films meeting the conditions laid down in Appendix II of the Council of Europe Agreement. A film qualified as 'a European cinematographic work' if it contained 'European elements' representing at least fifteen points out of a total of nineteen. These elements were weighted as follows:

- creative group (seven points) – director and scriptwriter (three points each), composer (one point)
- performing group (six points) – first role (three points), second role (two points), third role (one point) – determined by the number of days worked
- technical group (six points) – cameraman, sound recordist, editor, art director, studio or shooting location, and post-production location (one point each)

If a project failed to score fifteen points, it could still qualify if it was considered that the work reflected a European identity. The Convention had no language requirement and non-Council of Europe members could invest up to 30 per cent in projects.

The Convention was set up in order to encourage European co-production by providing a framework for enabling multilateral co-productions involving parties from three or more member states to access state subsidies in each of the countries concerned.

It could only enter into force once five states (at least four from the Council of Europe) had ratified it. Even though multilateral arrangements have become a common form of film financing, European producers did not rush to sign the Convention. It entered into force only on 1 April 1994 after Denmark, Switzerland, Sweden, Latvia and the UK had signed. One of the reasons for the Convention's early lack of appeal was that Eurimages, the Council of Europe's support programme, did not require co-productions to be made under the terms of the Convention in order to qualify for its funding. To date, the Convention appears to be most popular with those smaller European territories lacking a bilateral agreement with the larger countries.

Table 3.5 Co-productions (With All Foreign Partners) as Percentage of Total Productions (1988–98)

	1988	1994	1995	1996	1997	1998
Austria	11.1	30.0	5.3	13.3	20.0	41.7
Belgium	73.3	75.0	100.0	75.0	83.3	85.7
Denmark	12.5	21.4	30.8	38.1	30.4	66.7
Finland	21.4	36.4	50.0	20.0	10.0	87.5
France	32.1	47.0	55.3	44.8	47.2	44.3
Germany	14.0	19.3	41.3	34.4	23.0	25.2
Greece	6.7	83.3	94.4	50.0	62.5	
Ireland	60.0	11.8	18.2	66.7	27.3	
Italy	16.9	25.3	20.0	22.2	18.4	14.1
Luxembourg				100.0	100.0	
Netherlands	11.1	25.0	44.4	37.5	46.7	27.8
Portugal		77.8	78.6	75.0	30.8	
Spain	14.3	18.2	37.3	27.5	31.3	27.7
Sweden	33.3	24.0	86.7	83.3	13.8	35.0
UK	5.0	45.7	47.4	46.8	37.0	

Source: *Screen Digest* (1999a: 133)

Co-productions and/or co-financing arrangements now account for a significant proportion of productions in European territories (see table 3.5). Without co-productions, many small countries would not have a film industry. Co-productions have accounted for the majority of output from countries like Belgium, Greece, Ireland, Luxembourg and Portugal. With production and post-production costs rising throughout Europe, all countries have felt the need to spread the financial burden of film production.

Hoskins *et al.* (1997: 104) list the benefits of international co-productions:

- pooling of financial resources
- access to a foreign government's incentives and subsidies
- access to a partner's market
- access to a third-country market
- access to a project initiated by a partner
- cultural goals
- desired foreign locations
- cheaper inputs in a partner's country
- learning from a partner

Among the disadvantages of co-production are the increased costs incurred from co-ordinating the project, government red tape, loss of control and cultural specificity, opportunistic behaviour by the foreign partner, and the possibility that the partner may gain from the collaboration to become a formidable future competitor. Producers in the smaller countries are particularly concerned with the inflationary effects of co-productions. Sharon Strover (1994) also argues that the logistics of producing with foreign partners, 'particularly when they involve different languages and different industrial styles, creates pressures for certain styles of production and certain content at odds with anything distinctive or "national"'.

Widespread use of co-productions has led to the smaller territories frequently aligning themselves with a larger neighbour (e.g. France, Germany, Spain or the UK). While the Nordic countries continue to form a discrete group of their own, they are also linking with other regions both eastwards (Estonia, Hungary) and westwards (Scotland). Spain is now exploiting the large Spanish language/cultural market outside Europe by developing projects with Latin America.

In the UK, the advent of a European Co-production Fund in the early 1990s, together with the efforts of British Screen, may have done little to change the traditional attitude of UK producers to look for partners from across the Atlantic rather than the Channel. However, as European film financiers seek to back only those films with a significant prospect of recouping their investments, particularly films capable of entering the huge English-language market, the UK has become attractive to investors/producers from continental Europe.

Given France's generous system of subsidies and incentives, French producers have also been in strong demand as co-production partners, and occasionally, the CNC has had to intervene to ensure that all parties abide by the rules. In 1995, for instance, the imbalance between French and British investment saw co-productions between the two countries put on hold temporarily as the CNC insisted that the concept of 'reciprocity' be strictly applied.

East/West Partnerships

In the 1990s, international financing has become increasingly important to the film industries of Central and Eastern Europe. France is the main partner for Hungary, Romania and the Czech Republic. Poland's major co-production partner is Germany, and Greece is primarily involved with partners in the Balkans region (Iordanova, 1999a: 51). Yet, under the networking alliances that have emerged, some co-production partners are more capable of dictating the terms than others. According to Martin Ledinski, a delegate of the Young Hungarian Film-makers Association at an East–West Seminar held in Vienna in 1992, there are three types of co-productions between East and West. First, situations where Eastern European countries have no artistic input whatsoever and producers are used as mere suppliers of cheap facilities. Secondly, the so-called 'Euro-pudding', a hybrid mixing of artistic and cultural inputs, in which the use of a polyglot cast and international locations betrays the film's multinational sources of finance. Finally, the co-production of a subject-matter that is very particular to the East but has little chance of distribution in the West. With the third alternative, Western producers have tended to become interested only if the risks involved are covered under a government scheme or a European or pan-European fund.

In the territories in the former Eastern Bloc, the pace of change has been slow and the situation is far from uniform. 'The most successful film industries are still found in those countries where the democratic governments have displayed legislative and fiscal commitment' (Franklin, 1996: 22). For those industries, 'co-production and the assurance of foreign distribution it brings' are extremely important. According to the head of marketing at Space Films – and one of the leading producers and distributors of Czech films (including the 1997 Oscar and Golden Globe award-winner *Kolya*, see Chapter 4) – co-productions are 'the only commercially viable future for Czech films' (*ibid.*). With a little help from the West, investments in films made with local talent in Central and Eastern Europe are on the increase. However, to date, only the Russian director Nikita Mikhalkov has managed to raise a budget worthy of a Hollywood production. His film, *Sibirskij Tsiryulnik* (*The Barber of Siberia*) (1999), a French–Russian–Czech–Italian co-production shot in English and Russian, was reported to have cost US$49 million, two-thirds of which came from its French co-producer Michel Seydoux (Caméra One).

In 1990, France set up the ECO Fund (Fonds d'aide aux coproductions avec les pays d'Europe Centrale et Orientale) in order to help the struggling film industries of countries in the former Eastern Bloc. With an annual budget of around FF10 million, the ECO Fund contributed to the making of sixty-five feature films between 1990 and 1997 (see table 3.6).[8] Under French patronage, almost all ECO-supported films were shot on location in the country of the director and in a language other than French. For Romanian director Lucian

Table 3.6 ECO Fund-supported Films (1990–7)

	1990	1991	1992	1993	1994	1995	1996	1997
Number of Films	3	12	11	15	4	12	3	5
ECO Fund Support (FFm)	10	13	16	12	12	12	12	
Total French Investment (FFm)	17.37	53.45	57.59	50.10	21.43	48.59	14.96	15.54
Total Investment (FFm)					41.10	101.52	26.29	32.26

Source: *CNC Info* (2001b)

Pintilie (*Le Chêne* [*The Oak*] [1992 France/Romania]), Russian film-makers Vitali Kanievsky (*Samostoiatelnaia Jizn* [*An Independent Life*] [1992 France/Russia]) and Pavel Lounguine (*Luna Park* [1992 France/Russia]), and Lithuania's Sharunas Bartas (*Few of Us* [1996 Portugal/France/Germany/ Lithuania]), the fund represented a precious source of financing (Jäckel, 1997). Many ECO-supported films went on to win awards at various film festivals, both at home and abroad. In 1996, France announced its decision to put an end to the fund due to the existence of the pan-European Eurimages scheme, and the signs of recovery several countries were showing at the time.

English-language Production

There seems to be a growing consensus that the foundation of a competitive European industry depends on the capacity of producing higher budget pictures which can rely on recouping their costs from international territories. In the major and minor territories, the more commercially ambitious producers argue that the future lies in productions able to cross borders. As a result, investments in English-language productions have grown despite concern expressed by independent producers from non-English-language territories about loss of cultural specificity. Every significant film-producing country where English is not the first language is now making films in the English language. In many cases, the state is both directly and indirectly supporting the development of this internationally oriented cinema.

In the late 1980s and early 90s, a relaxation of French legislation towards English-language productions encouraged foreign producers to invest in large-budget French films involving British producers and American finance but with little French content. Examples include Jean-Jacques Annaud's *L'Ours* (*The Bear*) (1988 France), Luc Besson's *Le Grand bleu* (*The Big Blue*) (1988 France) and Ridley Scott's *1492, Conquest of Paradise*. Following protests from the French film industry, the legislation was tightened, only to be relaxed again a couple of years later to allow English-language pictures directed by French film-makers and with French technical and/or artistic input to be considered as 'French films'(with a reduced subsidy entitlement).[9] In 2000, ten 'French-initiated' films were made in the English language.

National and/or European legislation and directives have done little to prevent the major European players from making deals with American companies to invest large sums of money into productions with international appeal. German-based film funds have started to finance English-language films at a rate unknown in the past: between the end of 1999 and the autumn of 2000, the major fifteen private German-based investment funds (film and television) were reported to have co-produced or co-financed 124 American films for a total of

€1 million (Vital, 2001). Scandinavians are increasingly making films in English, and the larger Italian and Spanish players are also making and/or co-producing films in English.

European–American Co-production and Co-financing Arrangements

Despite vociferous protests against Hollywood domination and fears over the loss of creative control in films co-financed with American partners, Europe has generally welcomed American investment, and Europeans have invested both in American films and in the American film industry. With US distributors striving to retain their market share in overseas territories, most of the major American companies have now established production bases and deals in Europe. Along with high-profile movies, niche distributors (Miramax, Fox Searchlight, Paramount Classics, Sony Classics, Fine Line Features) are also working on and acquiring lower-budget foreign films. For example, in 1997, through its niche subsidiary Fox Searchlight, 20th Century-Fox financed the British-produced hit, *The Full Monty* (Peter Cattaneo 1997 UK/US). Disney has first-look deals in the UK, Germany, the Netherlands and Italy.

US companies have played a significant role in UK productions. Total investments in US/UK films reached a record high of £350.6 million in 1996. During 1999, American companies invested in nineteen films with a total combined budget of £303.64 million. Of this, £92 million was accounted for with the investments made by Universal Pictures and DreamWorks SKG in *Gladiator* (Ridley Scott 2000 US). A further estimated £50 million came from the United Artists backing for the James Bond movie *The World is Not Enough* (Michael Apted 1999 UK/US) from Eon Productions. DreamWorks has also signed a deal with Aardman Animations (UK) for all non-European rights to three animation films, starting with *Chicken Run* (Peter Lord and Nick Park 2000 UK/US). However, as UK industry observers have noted, American investment fluctuates due to multiple factors, particularly the exchange rate (Dyja, 1999: 23; Ilott, 1996: 27).

After the failure of French companies (Le Studio Canal Plus, Ciby 2000, Crédit Lyonnais) in Hollywood during the early 1990s, French conglomerates have changed tactics and developed close links with American partners to invest in 'global pictures'. Canal Plus has been the most ambitious in this enterprise: in 2000 the company formed an alliance with French distributor Bac Films, took control of Tobis in Germany, signed a first-look deal with Eclipse in Britain, and formed a joint venture with Michael Ovitz's Artists Production Group in the US (with a plan to produce fifteen films for the international market over the next three years). Since the merger of Canal Plus with Vivendi and Universal, French film executives at Vivendi Universal have claimed that more European talent will be used in films of worldwide appeal and more large-budget films shot in Europe with profits ploughed back into European film-making. Industry observers are now looking for signs of this promised development.

CONCLUSION

In 1989, Ian Christie suggested the unity to which the European film industries aspire should be a strategic one based upon 'commercial need' rather than a common culture (cited in Hill, 1994: 67). There is some evidence to suggest that this is becoming a reality. Co-financing arrangements, including co-productions made under official agreements and/or supported by the European (MEDIA) and pan-European (Eurimages) initiatives, have bolstered film production both in terms of output and budget. The accelerated development of pay television and video cassettes should provide European producers – as it did American producers in the last decades – with economic support for much greater increases in 'commercial' film production investment levels (Waterman and Jayakar, 2000: 504).

National government measures to help the film business have moved towards incentives rather than direct subsidies. This trend has boosted private investment in Europe's film industries. As *Screen Digest* (1999a: 119) noted:

> Governments have latched onto the reality that films are big business and excellent promotional tools for your country. A film economy is now a complex series of incentives and inducements, all attempting to entice an increasingly spoilt-for-choice set of producers, and further down the line to lure tourists as well.

Adoption of the euro should help investments even further: 'In the field of film production and distribution, Euro countries are more likely to collaborate with each other, increasing the ease in pursuing co-productions, joining forces and making sales to fellow Euro countries' (*Screen Digest*, 1999b: 263). For American and other foreign investors, the common currency will also reduce financial uncertainties inherent in floating exchange rates.

The next chapters will examine the role and impact of the European and pan-European financing initiatives set up in the late 1980s and the extent to which the current concentration and integration trends in Europe's distribution and exhibition networks benefit the European film industries.

NOTES

1. According to the Commission's estimates, an initial contribution of 90 million ecus from the Community budget was regarded as sufficient to guarantee financing projects until 2012/2013 (Bizern and Autissier, 1998: 85). Such a comprehensive approach was also preferred by the banking sector over 'the current piecing together of geographically restricted funds imposed by the compartmentalisation of national financial systems' (European Commission, 1997).

2. For a more complete survey of aid schemes in Germany, France, Italy, Spain and the UK, see Nikoltchev and Cabrera Blàzquez (2001).

3. The Producers Club also called for a 50 per cent quota system for showing European films on television (similar to the one proposed by the Television without Frontiers Directive), and co-production rules to be harmonised (based on a common definition of what constitutes a European film).

4. Canal Plus invested FF930 million in 140 films during 1999 (FF917.8 million in 117 films in 1998). Its rival TPS (in existence since 1997) invested FF104 million in nineteen films. Investments from the five terrestrial channels totalled FF557 million (641 in 1998) (*CNC Info*, 2000: 43).

5. In 1998, ARTE invested FF49.7 million in twenty-one feature films (Dubet, 2000: 226).

6. France has over forty cinematographic co-production agreements with countries all around the world. However outdated official co-production treaties may be, countries – with the major exception of the US – continue to sign inter-governmental agreements. In the 1990s, Ireland signed an agreement with France, while others (including Belgium, Italy and the UK), have revised their co-production treaties to allow co-financing arrangements.

7. If a bilateral agreement exists between two countries, it still applies. If a project involves more than two producers from different member states, the Convention overrides any bilateral agreements.

8. French co-operation with Eastern Europe was not totally disinterested, since under ECO rules, French financing would go to the French production company and/or post-production would be done in French studios.

9. This has brought fears that the French fund would not only finance films that 'do not reflect French creativity and culture' but that it would also become a financing resource centre for French and foreign business interests (Danan, 1996: 80–1).

4

European and Pan-European Production Initiatives

As the previous chapter showed, film production in Europe is heavily reliant on state-aid mechanisms, tax incentives and television finance. The case for state intervention has been widely made, and public support, at regional and national levels, continues to be fundamental to building up and maintaining a local film industry.

The late 1980s were marked by the creation of programmes at European (MEDIA, EUREKA Audiovisual) and pan-European (Eurimages) levels. These initiatives were set up to help establish networks and mobilise capital resources through partnerships in the audiovisual industries. Renewed interest in the European film industries and the devising of European film and audiovisual policy in the 1980s originated from concerns over:

- rapidly developing new technologies
- the increasing number and popularity of American films and television programmes shown on European screens
- the prospect of a unified Europe (with a market of 320 million people)

With the last point, Europe's film and audiovisual sector was seen as a decisive factor in achieving European unification by, among others, the President of the Commission of the European Community, Jacques Delors.

This chapter examines the role of European and pan-European programmes aimed at developing Europe's film industries since the late 1980s, exploring the evolution of the European Community's MEDIA programme and the Council of Europe's Eurimages fund. Following the developments observed in the previous chapters, it also discusses the implications of the recent trend to view cultural justifications for film policy increasingly as part of a wider competitiveness policy (Pratten and Deakin, 2000: 222). The chapter also explores the extent to which some harmonisation has occurred as a result of these European intitiaves.

THE MEDIA PROGRAMME

The First Five Years

The European Community's MEDIA programme was instigated in 1987 to aid and encourage initiatives designed to fulfil the needs of the entire audiovisual sector and to protect minority languages. Ten pilot projects were set up in 1987–8 for an experimental period of three years. The initial investment in 1988 was small: a budget of 5.5 million ecus financed projects (the overall value of those MEDIA-financed projects was estimated at 15 million ecus). More than 2,000 companies and organisations participated in the preparation of the projects.

Following this pilot phase, in October 1990 the Commission's President, Jacques Delors, requested a budget of 250 million ecus for the next stage of the programme. In December 1990, MEDIA was given the go-ahead by the Council of Ministers, with a budget of 200 million ecus (£140 million) to be spread over five years. MEDIA became a fully fledged Community programme, with twelve projects covering:

- professional training – EAVE (European Audiovisual Entrepreneurs) based in Brussels and the MEDIA Business School based in Madrid
- development and production – SCRIPT (the European Script Fund) based in London, CARTOON (to support the creation and development of animation) in Brussels, DOCUMENTARY shared between Copenhagen and Amsterdam, and the MEDIA Investment Club and MAP-TV (to develop audiovisual production of documentaries using archive material) both at Bry-sur-Marne in France
- distribution – EFDO (European Film Distribution Office) in Hamburg, EVE (Espace Video Européen) in Dublin, GRECO (Groupement de Circulation des Oeuvres Européennes) in Munich and Paris, and EURO AIM (European Organisation for an Audiovisual Independent Market) in Brussels
- dubbing and subtitling – BABEL (Broadcasting Across the Barriers of European Language) in Geneva

The aim was 'to create cross-border synergies' by establishing networks of co-operation and exchange and by mobilising capital resources through partnerships. MEDIA could not contribute more than 50 per cent of the total cost for any single project; the rest came from private and/or public sources. Located in various European territories, the MEDIA projects were managed by industry professionals, with the European Commission merely acting as a political and economic facilitator.

In 1993, the MEDIA programme was given a clean bill of health in Roland Berger's interim report (Berger, 1993), which offered a powerful argument for extending support to and beyond 1995. By then, the twelve MEDIA initiatives had grown to nineteen. They now also included initiatives for:

- exhibition – MEDIA Salles in Milan, EUROPA CINEMAS in Paris and the EFA (the European Film Academy, responsible for the European film awards) in Berlin
- stimulation of financial investment – EURO MEDIA Garanties (EGM) based in Paris
- conservation and restoration of films – LUMIERE in Lisbon
- development and production – SOURCES (Stimulating Outstanding Resources for Creative European Screenwriting) in Amsterdam, and SCALE (Small Countries improve their Audiovisual Level in Europe) in Lisbon

The Berger report made several recommendations, among which were a better pre-selection of films and more support for films with higher budgets. It had registered several complaints about management accountability (including excessive operating costs) and transparency. Other criticisms included duplication of resources and a lack of mechanisms for the recoupment of loans.

Table 4.1 Market Share of Domestic Films in European Countries (1989–2000)
(%)[1]

	1989	1990	1991	1992	1993	1994	1995	1996	1997	1998	1999	2000
Belgium	0.4	1.4	2.2	5.0	1.6	1.1	0.3	0.1	0.9	0.5		1.0
Denmark	15.0	14.7	10.8	15.3	15.9	21.5	8.3	17.2	19.0	14.4	28.8	
Finland	7.4	13.9	13	10.9	6.3	4.0	11.2	3.5	5.6	10.4		
France*	34.3	37.5	30.6	35.0	35.1	28.3	35.2	37.5	34.5	27.6	32.4	28.5
Germany	16.7	9.7	13.6	9.5	7.2	10.1	6.3	15.3	17.3	8.1	14.0	12.2
Greece	9.0	8.0	7.0	2.0					4.0			
Ireland	4.0	5.0	2.0									
Italy	21.7	21.0	26.8	24.4	17.3	23.7	21.1	24.9	32.9	24.7	24.1	17.5
Luxembourg	2.0	2.0	2.0	0.0	0.8	0.1	0.0		1.7	0.5		
Netherlands	4.6	3.0	2.3	13.0	4.1	0.6	7.6	5.4	3.4	6.1	5.3	
Portugal	1.2	2.2	2.1	2.0	1.0				2.0	6.9		
Spain	7.4	10.4	10.9	9.3	8.8	7.1	12.2	9.3	13.1	11.9	13.8	10.0
Sweden	20.4	10.4	25.6	17.0	20.3	19.9	20.1	18.0	17.8	16.0		
UK	10.0	7.0	6.8	2.5	8.8	12.3	10.2	12.8	28.1	14.2	17.8	21.0

Sources: *CNC Info* (2001b); EAO (2001a)

Note:
1. Shares include co-productions.

Table 4.2 Market Shares of US Films in European Countries (1989–2000)
(%)

	1989	1990	1991	1992	1993	1994	1995	1996	1997	1998	1999	2000
Belgium	68.4	79.1	78.6	69.3	75.8	72.4	69.7	73.7	71.9	70.9	78.3	70.0 [1]
Denmark	63.7	77.0	83.3	77.7	74.1	66.5	81.1	67.1	65.5	74.1	57.0	
Finland	70.0	80.0	80.0	63.0	63.0	66.0	76.5	75.2	73.1			
France*	55.5	55.9	58.0	58.2	57.1	60.9	53.9	54.3	52.2	63.2	53.9	62.9
Germany	65.7	83.9	80.2	82.8	87.8	81.6	87.1	75.1	70.5	85.4	76.5	
Greece	86.0	87.0	88.0	92.0								
Ireland	85.0	87.0	91.5									
Italy	63.1	70.0	58.6	59.4	70.0	61.1	63.2	59.7	46.7	63.8	53.1	70.0
Luxembourg	87.0	80.0	85.0	78.0	80.0	84.0	82.4	78.5	68.4	80.7		
Netherlands	75.6	85.8	92.5	78.8	89.3	89.9	82.0	89.7	84.5	88.7	75.1	
Portugal	67.4	63.5	67.8	68.4	97.0	95.0			66.5	68.5		
Spain	71.4	72.5	68.7	77.1	75.7	72.3	71.9	78.2	68.2	78.5	64.4	81.6
Sweden	69.3	82.3	70.5	65.5	73.6	67.5	68.5	65.9	67.5	66.7	43.0	
UK	86.2	88.0	89.0	92.5	94.2	85.6	85.2	81.7	69.3	83.9	80.5	75.3

Sources: *CNC Info* (2001b); EAO (2001a)

Note:
1. Brussels only.

MEDIA was also criticised for being too fragmented – a number of producers claimed they found it difficult to identify programmes to which they could apply – and for spreading its resources too thinly. In addition, it was alleged that MEDIA suffered from internal divisions. Despite these criticisms, the MEDIA programme was considered a success and continued to be held in high regard by many inside the industry.[1]

By 1995, however, in all European territories, domestic productions had not succeeded in securely increasing their market share (see table 4.1), and US films continued to dominate overwhelmingly (see table 4.2). MEDIA's overall objective of promoting and strengthening the competitiveness of Europe's film and television industries therefore remained unfulfilled. Problems resulted from incompatibility between Community and national schemes, together with mistrust among EU members and their opposed visions (Collins, 1999: 198). Also, as John Hill (1994: 67) points out, the main thrust of the MEDIA programme at the time seemed to be 'less concerned with forging a supranational industry than with "promoting ... national industries at Community level" through various forms of assistance', particularly in the support given to the distribution and exhibition of national films across borders. Nonetheless, at the end of its initial five-year term, MEDIA seemed to have achieved one of its major goals: the creation of networks of co-operation and understanding between producers from different member states.

MEDIA II

Reviewed in 1995, the MEDIA initiatives were trimmed down and the programme renamed MEDIA II. France had requested 400 million ecus, but the
final budget was fixed at 310 million ecus over a five-year period (1996–2000).
In a larger European Union (the fifteen EU member states plus Iceland and
Norway), MEDIA II was to concentrate its efforts on the:

- continuous training of European audiovisual professionals
- development of projects and companies
- transnational circulation of European film and television works

In the field of cinema, it was believed achievements in these three areas would
help to attain the following ultimate objectives:

- strengthen the European industry's competitiveness by supporting the
  development of projects with a genuine potential for distribution
- respect for linguistic and cultural diversity
- develop the potential of countries or regions with low production capacity
  and restricted geographic areas or linguistic populations
- the development of a sector of independent production and distribution
  companies, consisting mainly of small and medium-sized companies (BIPE
  Conseil, 1998: 26)

MEDIA II was more centralised and less controlled by industry professionals
than its predecessor. Following a process of tendering, four contracted intermediary organisations were selected to provide technical assistance on behalf of
the Commission but had no decision-making powers when it came to payments
or the selection of beneficiaries. Projects were first evaluated by the intermediary
organisations and a panel of experts, before selections were made by the Commission assisted by the MEDIA Committee (made up of two or three
representatives from each of the states participating in the programme and
chaired by the Commission representative).

MEDIA II was more economically directed and less culturally oriented than
its predecessor. With a focus on distribution, MEDIA II emphasised the development of films and television programmes likely to cross borders and attract a
large share of their audience in the larger European market. MEDIA II encouraged production companies to develop whole slates of films rather than single
projects and stressed the importance of establishing a business plan. These new
requirements resulted in a sharp fall in the number of applications (from 349 to
49) made between 1996 and 1997.

With a larger share of the budget allocated to distribution, the short- and medium-term objectives of MEDIA II were to encourage distributors to increase their investment in – and handling of – more European films. Grants were also available to promote films at the various markets and festivals, capped at 50 per cent of the cost of promotion. A new line of support for the distribution of European films within Europe was set up in 1996. Support for dubbing and subtitling also remained important. Support for exhibition continued under the Media Salles and EUROPA CINEMAS schemes (see pages 82–4).

MEDIA representatives from the ten smaller European Union member states (Austria, Belgium, Denmark, Finland, Greece, Ireland, Luxembourg, the Netherlands, Portugal and Sweden) successfully campaigned to get the guidelines for distribution support changed. The MEDIA programme is now committed to favouring projects from 'countries or regions with low production capacity and/or restricted geographical and linguistic areas'. One effect of this positive discrimination is that before committing to a film, distributors want to know the European nationality of the film to determine whether their risk might be covered by MEDIA support (BIPE Conseil, 1998: 164).

Under the distribution action line of MEDIA II, selective support (in the form of a repayable loan based on the net box-office takings of a film's distributors) became available for the release of non-national European (N-NE) films.[2] To be entitled to this aid (capped for each distributor at 125,000 ecus per film within a limit of 50 per cent of the distribution budget), a film had to have a marketing plan and be released by three distributors in different European countries. In 1996, Jacques Delmoly, head of the MEDIA programme, announced that in its first year of operation, this new action line involved 240 distribution plans covering thirty-seven selected films. A mid-term evaluation of MEDIA II by BIPE Conseil (BIPE Conseil, 1998) found that among countries with a small volume of production, Danish and Dutch films circulated better than others. Support per film varied between 25,000 ecus for *Out of the Present* (Andrei Vjica 1996 Germany/France/Belgium/Russia) and 627,000 ecus for *Breaking the Waves*, both from Denmark (p. 177).[3]

In accordance with EU Council's recommendations, the MEDIA programme was enlarged and made accessible to non-EU countries under certain conditions to be arranged by the parties concerned with the:

- participation of the 'Associated Countries' of Central and Eastern Europe (Hungary, Poland, the Czech Republic, Slovakia, Bulgaria and Romania)
- participation of Cyprus, Malta and L'Association européenne de libre-échange (AELE) states that are members of the European Economic Area (EEA) agreement

- collaboration of other third-party countries that have reached agreements on media legislation

By the end of the 1990s, lengthy bilateral negotiations between the Commission and the authorities of the countries regarded as suitable for joining the programme had not yet resulted in those countries having any effective participation (Bizern and Autissier, 1998: 82).

Results of MEDIA II

As MEDIA II drew to a close, the European Commission issued statistics detailing the achievements of the programme. Over the course of its five years, MEDIA II assisted the development of 1,690 European film and audiovisual works (television series, documentaries, animation, multimedia works) and 281 production companies (UK MEDIA Desk, 2001). Support for development benefited some of Europe's best-known directors, including Lars von Trier, Istvan Szabo, Terence Davies, Fridrick Thor Fridrikson and Gérard Corbiau, together with lesser-known directors such as Damien O'Donnell (*East is East* 1999 UK), Shekhar Kapur (*Elizabeth* 1998 UK) and Karim Dridi (*Hors jeu* 1998 France).

Like its predecessor, MEDIA II set up a number of training programmes and workshops designed to improve the skills of a large number of European professionals (producers, screenwriters, script-editors, development executives, new media developers, etc.). The films benefiting from these training initiatives include award-winners like *Breaking the Waves*, *Antonia's Line* (Marleen Gorris 1995 Netherlands/Belgium/UK), *Death and the Maiden* (Roman Polanski 1995

East is East (1999)

UK/US/France), *To Vlemma tou Odyssea* (*Ulysses' Gaze*) and *Ma vie en rose*. Between 1996 and 1997, MEDIA II training initiatives made it possible to establish partnerships with more than 400 institutions (production companies, professional associations, training centres) in seventeen countries (BIPE Conseil, 1998: 66). On average, MEDIA II supported 145 training initiatives per year. Of these, the best attended were in the areas of management (44.8 per cent), new technologies (39.7 per cent) and scriptwriting (15.5 per cent). The UK had the largest number of participants, followed by France, Italy, Germany, Greece, Spain, Finland, the Netherlands, Belgium, Ireland, Sweden, Portugal, Denmark, Norway, Austria, Luxembourg and Iceland (*Informations Programme MEDIA*, 2001: 4).

MEDIA II financially supported the promotion and distribution of 400 European films. Other MEDIA II support went to festivals and audiovisual events. It also supported 275 television programmes, 200 video catalogues of European works, and 350 cinemas showing European films to an audience of more than 75 million all over Europe (*MEDIA France Bulletin*, 2000a). The number of European films distributed outside their country of origin increased from 246 films in 1996, to 456 in 1999. In relation to the number of films produced in Europe during the same period, the percentage of films distributed outside their country of origin rose from 13.7 per cent to 22.2 per cent (UK MEDIA Desk, 2001).

Criticisms of MEDIA II included the withdrawal of EU support in the area of production, despite conditions set for distributors to reinvest the automatic aid in production, and a lack of initiative in the domain of export (Dubet, 2000: 178). It was also felt that training initiatives offered far too many courses. In some territories, the programme was also criticised for favouring larger companies rather than creative individuals, and the use of only two languages (English and French) in a number of official documents was regarded as benefiting the larger countries.

MEDIA Plus

In 1999, the European Commission allocated a budget of €400 million (around £240 million) over five years (1 January 2001–31 December 2005) to MEDIA Plus, the successor of MEDIA II.[4] Raising the programme's budget was justified by the Commission because of:

- a greater consideration of the specific needs of the industries in countries with lower audiovisual capacity and/or restricted geographical and linguistic area
- the increased use of automatic support mechanisms based on market performance

- the emergence of new needs and projects linked to the development of new technologies
- the predominance which needed to be given to the transnational circulation of European audiovisual works, within and outside the European Union (Commission of the European Communities, 1999: 5–6)

Smaller countries, including Austria, Denmark, Ireland and the Netherlands, had lobbied for more money to be spent on development, but other members (notably France) were unwilling to support an increase in development funding. Stalemate over the budget ended only in November 2000. The French approach not only clashed with that of the smaller countries with little funding of their own for development, but also with the British position, which was strongly in favour of supporting slates of projects rather than individual films.

After much discussion, EU culture ministers voted unanimously to accept the €400 million budget. This was allocated as follows:

- 57.5 per cent for distribution
- 20 per cent for development (€80 million, increasing from €58.9 million under MEDIA II)
- 8.5 per cent for promotion (separated from distribution)
- 5 per cent for pilot projects (to encourage the transition to digital technology)
- 9 per cent for 'horizontal costs' (the running of MEDIA Plus information desks)

Support was offered in the form of repayable loans and a secondary scheme based on admissions from European films outside their country of origin. Independent production companies could apply for up to 50 per cent of their development costs for projects. Funding was made available for single projects or slates of projects. Script awards were expected to be 'as automatic as possible' and it was anticipated that the proportion of state funding would be higher, with slates only awarded to producers with at least three international releases. Eligibility criteria included the track record of the company, the project's potential in the international marketplace, and the availability of match funding. For training, MEDIA Plus introduced the possibility of organisations submitting grouped applications and the option of contracts extending over successive years for existing training providers (*MEDIA England Bulletin*, 2001).

After progress was hampered by lengthy delays in the implementation of the new programme during the transition period, industry professionals were relieved when the increased MEDIA budget was passed under the French presidency of the European Union. Those critics who deplored the protectionist stance of much European policy in the past, welcomed what they called a 'new aggressiveness' on the part of EU policy-makers. However, many people thought that the budget did not endow the MEDIA programme with resources commensurate to the size, scope and strategic importance of the industry. The International Federation of Film Distributors Association was the first to criticise the new budget as too low. Innovations, such as support for music recording and special effects, did not meet with unanimous approval either. There were also concerns expressed about proposals for allocating funding to promote Europe's sales agencies and pilot projects for multimedia work, such as the digitisation of archives. Also, fears arose that the new international direction given to the programme may not necessarily contribute towards promoting Europe's cultural diversity and might even jeopardise some of the gains secured so far by previous phases of the programme.

EURIMAGES

Early Years

Arguably the programme that has most emphasised the cultural importance of film is not MEDIA but the Council of Europe's fund for co-production, Eurimages. European identity and the cultural nature of the programme were highlighted by Eurimages' president Gaetano Adinolfi in 1991 when he talked of 'the eminent cultural nature of the Fund, whose main objective is to support works which uphold the values that are part and parcel of European identity' (*Forum du Conseil de l'Europe*, 1991: 43). In 1993, Eurimages' executive secretary Ryclef Rienstra described the main aim of the fund as 'not to get its money back but to support an activity which is both industrial and cultural, and which asserts Europe's identity' (*Forum du Conseil de l'Europe*, 1993: 41). While there has been no attempt to define such an identity beyond general references to diversity and common cultural heritage, many films supported by Eurimages in the early 1990s tackled contemporary issues (e.g. of belonging, or not belonging) and explored cross-cultural exchanges (Jäckel, 2000).

Eurimages was set up in 1988. First discussed within the framework of the MEDIA programme, the programme was developed within the Council of Europe. A French initiative (France allocated half the initial budget), it was intended to group public funding from the twelve founding members to foster the co-production and distribution of cinematographic works (both fiction and documentary) between European partners. Initially, participation in the programme involved ten EC countries, without Ireland and the UK, and two non-EC members, Austria and Switzerland. By 1991, Eurimages had nineteen members. The UK joined in 1993 before withdrawing in 1996 despite protests from British producers. The amount of contributions was left to the discretion of its member states but took into account the official scale of contributions set by the Council of Europe (loosely determined according to a formula based on GNP and population). Eurimages' resources were made up from annual contributions by the fund's member states and associate member states, together with the amount of repaid loans and any other payments, donations or legacies agreed by the board of management.

The overall structure of Eurimages has remained largely unchanged. The Strasbourg-based fund is managed by a board to which every Eurimages member state appoints a representative. In reaching decisions on financial assistance, the board takes account of the artistic quality of a project and the professional standing of the key individuals involved. Between meetings of the board, the chairman is responsible for the implementation of the fund's policies. The secretariat, led by an executive secretary, organises the meetings of the board and follows its decisions (Bizern and Autissier, 1998: 70).

Projects are supported in the form of conditional interest-free loans referred to as 'advances on receipts'. Producers pay back the sums they receive when the film makes a profit. Eurimages' co-production funding is normally allocated once a film has 50 per cent of financing already in place. As such, it often acts as a financial guarantee in the sense that it helps producers find additional financing or new approaches to film financing (p. 71). The Eurimages board pays particular attention to projects originating in member states with low cinematographic production levels and to co-productions that bring together co-producers from states with high and low production levels.

Originally, a minimum of three co-producers from member states (two for documentaries) had to be involved in order for a film to qualify for Eurimages support. Producers from non-member states were allowed, but their participation was limited to 30 per cent of the film budget (compared to 60 – increased to 70 per cent in 1994 – for the majority producer, and 20 – decreased to 10 – per cent for the minority producer of a member state). Since 1998, the fund has been open to bilateral films. Similar rules apply to the support given to distributors and exhibitors in the form of loans covering dubbing, subtitling and the supply of prints.

At first the fund supported only low- and medium-budget films. Between 1989 and 1992, Eurimages helped produce 144 feature films. Total production costs of both fiction and documentary films was 469 million ecus, of which 11 per cent was financed by the fund.[5] Films benefiting from this funding included Xavier Koller's *Reise der Hoffnung* (*Journey of Hope*) (1990 Switzerland/UK), Lars von Trier's *Europa* (1991 Denmark/Sweden/France/Germany), Gianni

Amelio's *Il Ladro di bambini* (*The Stolen Children*) (1992 France/Italy), Jaco van
Dormael's *Toto le héros* (1991 France/Belgium/Germany), Fernando Trueba's
Belle époque (1992 Spain/Portugal/France), Krzysztof Kieślowski's *Trois
couleurs: Bleu* (1993 France/Poland/Switzerland) and aid for the distribution of
Nikita Mikhalkov's *Urga* (1991 France/Soviet Union). Early success was evident
in the increasing number of applications made to the fund, and in 1994 it was
estimated that of all films made in Europe that year, over a quarter had received
Eurimages support (*Eurimages News*, 1994). Growth in co-productions involving European partners was largely responsible for the upward path taken by
European production in the early 1990s (see table 3.2 on page 48).[6]

Mid-term Assessment and Evolution of Eurimages

Eurimages aims to promulgate 'European values and identities' but also to
strengthen Europe's film industries. However, the programme's meagre
resources have not enabled it to become a major contributor to advancing the
competitiveness of those industries. In 1995, the fund made awards totalling 22
million ecus, a very small amount in comparison to the 130 million ecus of direct
aid France granted to its film industry in the same year (Eurocinéma, 1996:
18–19).[7] Film budgets have fluctuated over the years, making it difficult to find
a pattern, but the amounts of money loaned by Eurimages have risen steadily.

Eurimages has often been criticised for its poor record in recouping its loans.
Defending the programme in 1995, Barrie Ellis-Jones, the fund's British chief
executive, explained that 'a very large proportion of the money had gone to co-
productions coming out of smaller countries'. 'They are inevitably the ones that
struggle in the market-place and are unlikely to recoup quickly', he said (quoted
in Finney, 1996: 110). Eurimages' contributions seemed to illustrate that economic and cultural development approaches to cinema could be reconciled. As
David Hancock (1996: 11) pointed out:

> the progress shown in film by producers from small linguistic or cultural areas
> [shows] that, with a strong commitment, clear policy and the political will,
> successful films can be made almost anywhere, even from areas with a relatively
> small funding base.

A 1998 assessment of the programme found that Eurimages' involvement in
European feature film co-productions had grown from 17 per cent in 1989 to
46 per cent in 1996. For countries with low production capacity, like Iceland,
Luxembourg, Turkey and Hungary, the report stated that Eurimages had
become 'an indispensable additional element in completing the financing of feature films' (Bizern and Autissier, 1998: 70).

During the period in which the UK participated in the programme, nearly a third of all UK films made in 1994 and 1995 received Eurimages' support. Arguing to retain membership of the fund, UK producers pointed out that in a period of just under three years, for their government's £5.5 million contribution to Eurimages, £12.5 million had been invested in UK co-productions, generating £40 million worth of film-making activity.[8] The (sudden) announcement of the UK's withdrawal in 1996 had an impact on the overall conduct of the fund. In 1992, the Eurimages board had taken the decision to make production loans only to projects shot in the language of the co-producers in participating member states. The UK's withdrawal disappointed many continental producers, for British membership had made possible participation in Eurimages-funded English-language productions. However, the decision on language was subsequently reversed and several films supported by the fund were made in English, even before Ireland joined the fund.

Since 1 January 2000, new regulations have entered into force and support is granted according to two schemes. Under the first of these, projects are evaluated on their 'international circulation potential', with awards made of up to FF4 million for films with an estimated budget of under FF35 million or FF5 million for projects with a budget over FF35 million. Projects must have 75 per cent of their financing already in place and be distributed in a minimum of three countries. The second scheme is aimed at supporting 'the cultural and economic diversity of European cinema', aiding 'films of artistic value'. To be eligible, a project has to have 50 per cent of financing in place, and Eurimages offers maximum funding of FF2.5 million to films with an estimated budget of under FF20 million, while those with a budget over FF20 million are eligible for a maximum award of FF3 million (*Eurimages News*, 2000). The choice to enter a film in the first or second category rests with the producer. Eurimages support is now open to all bilateral co-productions made under a co-production agreement, even to films for which one co-producer is only a financial partner.

Since the implementation of the new schemes, the awards made have not indicated any major departure from Eurimages' original remit to support culturally significant works. Films directed by Istvan Szabo (Hungary), Ettore Scola (Italy) and French New Wave veteran Jacques Rivette were selected under the first category.

Eurimages and the Industries of Central and Eastern Europe

The pan-European programmes acknowledge the problems faced in the smaller territories, particularly those in Eastern Europe. Eurimages has proposed to set up a network of cinemas by providing financial support to exhibitors in European countries that do not have access to MEDIA initiatives. To qualify for the aid, at least 33 per cent of films shown by exhibitors from Bulgaria, Cyprus, the Czech Republic, Hungary, Poland, Slovakia, Switzerland and Turkey must be European.

With extremely modest resources at its disposal, Eurimages in the last decade has played the role of life-saver to many films from Central and Eastern Europe. Yet Eurimages' role in those countries has recently come under attack for its sporadic and selective approach to the cinemas of the region. Dina Iordanova (2002b) believes that the divorce of production assistance from distribution has been particularly detrimental to the industries in those territories. She deplores how, in early 2000, of the ten projects supported that involved Eastern European directors, only one was co-produced by an Eastern European country. Iordanova therefore argues that after a brief period of interest in Eastern Europe, Eurimages now concentrates almost exclusively on Western European priorities. She further suggests the belief of Eurimages' administrators that film-makers should be able to at least secure the release of their films in their own countries is detrimental to the distribution of Eastern European films:

> As a result of [Eurimages'] philosophy, many films never go into distribution in all their co-production partner countries. This is particularly true for the minority co-producers: films, which involve the creative potential and force of a small film industry, never become part of their own national cinematic culture. Bulgaria, for example, is a minority producer of a number of films that have never been seen in the country (p. 531).

She suggests that the fund should 'support distribution in the countries where the film is likely to be seen' (p. 531) (those of the co-producers included) and commit itself to aiding the distribution of films it has helped produce.

It is evident that the film industries of the former Eastern Bloc need special treatment in the particularly difficult transition from state control to a market economy. However, to blame these problems on Eurimages seems unfair since the fund has taken a leading but limited role in encouraging the circulation of films from Central and Eastern Europe. Theatrical release is a major problem for European film. Cultural affinities do not always help the circulation of films across borders. Iordanova admits that in the East, the situation is 'partially due to the mere lack of interest by Eastern European distributors in the cinematic output of their neighbours' (p. 533). To suggest Eurimages should concentrate support on the distribution of European films in their domestic territories would indicate a profound and controversial departure from the objectives of initiatives primarily aimed at fostering co-operation and exchange among Europeans.

CASE STUDY: *KOLYA*

Given the UK government's antipathy towards Eurimages, it is ironic that *Kolya*, one of the programme's most commercially and critically successful projects, should have been initiated by a British producer. The film, from the Czech director Jan Sverák, was partly funded through the programme. In 1994, British producer Eric Abraham's Portobello Pictures had already made a Czech film, Jirí Menzel's *Zivot a neobycejnác dobrodruzství vojáka Ivana Conkina* (*The Life and Extraordinary Adventures of Private Ivan Chonkin*) (1994 Czech Republic/UK/France/Italy/Russia), before backing the production of *Kolya*. At the script stage, the French co-producer Pandora Cinéma SA became involved, and with that commitment came the support of the French ECO Fund (see Chapter 3) and Eurimages. A co-production involving companies and cast from four countries, *Kolya* manages to avoid the pitfalls inherent in multinational deals.

The majority of the £850,000 budget came from Czech sources, including contributions from Biograf, Sverák's own company, the television network CZTV for television rights, theatrical distributor Lucerna Film (equity investment), and pre-sales to CCV (video rights) and Cinemart, as well as the support of the State Fund of the Czech Republic for the Support and Development of Czech Cinematography. Eurimages' contribution to the production of *Kolya* was FF1 million in 1995.

Kolya (1996)

By the time Jan Sverák made *Kolya*, the thirty-one-year-old director had established himself as the most versatile and successful of the new Czech film-makers. In 1989, his 'Sci-fi-ecology' documentary, *Oil Gobblers*, had received the prestigious Los Angeles AMPAS Student Oscar for best foreign film. Sverák's debut feature, *Obecná Skola* (*The Elementary School*) (1991 Czecho-slovakia) was nominated in 1992 for the Best Foreign Film at the Academy Awards. His next two films, *Akumulàtor I* (1994 Czech Republic) and *Jizda* (*The Ride*) (1995 Czech Republic), were also hits with Czech audiences.

Despite its Oscar nomination, *Obecná Skola* had not found a distributor out-side the Czech Republic. To ensure *Kolya* was seen in several countries, Sverák created his own production company, Biograf Jan Sverák Film. With *Kolya*, the touching story of a five-year-old Russian boy who transforms the life of a crusty middle-aged Czech bachelor, Jan Sverák found the global audience he was seek-ing. When *Kolya* was screened at the Cannes film market in 1996, seventeen distributors, including Miramax, rushed to acquire the various rights of the film. The film was released in forty countries worldwide. By 1997, it had sold more than 1.3 million tickets in its home country, with 1.4 million admissions in the Euro-pean Union and 1.2 million in the US. In the Czech Republic, *Kolya* was the most popular film of 1996, taking almost twice as much as the nearest rival, *Indepen-dence Day* (Roland Emmerich 1996 US), that year. The film won the 1997 Academy and Golden Globe awards for best non-English-language film. Sverák's film also won six Czech Lion awards (including Best Picture and Best Director), the 1997 UN award Time for Peace, the Grand Prix at the 1996 International Fes-tival Tokyo award, and several other prizes at international film festivals around the world.

CASE STUDY: EUROPA CINEMAS

Eurimages has supported not only the production but also the exhibition of European films. EUROPA CINEMAS was established in 1992 as a network of film theatres encouraging the programming of European films within Europe. Based in Paris, EUROPA CINEMAS is supported by MEDIA and Eurimages, together with the European Commission, the CNC, EUREKA Audiovisuel and the French Ministry of Foreign Affairs (Paris). The budget of EUROPA CIN-EMAS has gone from €800,000 in its first year of operation, to €4.3 million in 1999. At the same time, the network has grown from eighty-two screens at thirty-two sites in twelve countries, to 831 screens (350 sites) in thirty-nine European countries (EUROPA CINEMAS, 2000: 3).

The level of support given to exhibitors is determined by the percentage of European films screened in their theatres, with priority going to non-domestic productions, along with the total number of screens operated by the same theatre and the market share of European films in the country. Those receiving support were required to:

- sign a minimum six-month contract to provide European programming
- set up initiatives aimed at young audiences
- report programme information and participate in joint network activities via the Internet
- submit every six months a detailed report including the title, number of screenings, admissions and box-office takings for every film shown

In 1999, exhibitors working as part of the network programmed 64.14 per cent of European films (58.8 per cent in 1998), of which 40.5 per cent were films from outside the host nation (35 per cent in 1998). They registered 19.8 million admissions for European films (15.5 million in 1998), generating box-office takings of €100 million. 12.7 million admissions (8.8 million in 1998) were for non-domestic productions. At the end of 1999, the films with the highest non-domestic admissions in EUROPA CINEMAS theatres were *La vita è bella* (*Life is Beautiful*) (1.35 million outside Italy), *Festen* (*The Celebration*) (Thomas Vinterberg 1998 Denmark) (840,000 admissions outside Denmark) and *Todo sobre mi madre* (*All About My Mother*) (Pedro Almodóvar 1999 Spain/France) (685,000 admissions outside Spain).

EUROPA CINEMAS' support is not limited to exhibitors in EU countries. Activities now extend to the countries in the former Eastern Bloc, and since March 2000, EUROPA CINEMAS also operates a Mediterranean network (EUROMED) with a budget of €4 million over a three-year period. EUROMED partners include the fifteen EU countries and twelve Mediterranean countries (Algeria, Cyprus, Egypt, Israel, Jordan, Lebanon, Malta, Morocco, the Palestinian territories, Syria, Tunisia and Turkey). The aims of EUROMED are for the:

- twelve Mediterranean partners 'to reinforce the structures of diffusion and increase the share of European and Mediterranean films in the programming of cinemas by supporting exhibitors, distributors and festival directors in these markets'
- EU countries 'to develop a cinema network at an international level by uniting professionals from the cinema sector around common aims for a better circulation of Mediterranean and European films' (EUROPA CINEMAS/ EUROMED, 2000: 1)

Table 4.3 Market Share of Films by Nationality in EUROPA CINEMAS Network Theatres (1999–2000)

(%)

	1999	2000
USA	30	40
France	16	15
United Kingdom	14	11
Spain	8	4
Italy	7	5
Germany	6	4
Denmark	4	
Other European	8	13
Other non-European	7	8

Sources: EUROPA CINEMAS (2000 and 2001)

After just over a year of operation, Claude-Eric Poiroux, the general director of EUROPA CINEMAS, claimed that EUROMED support already had 'a deep impact in regions where cinema was becoming an endangered species or Hollywood mono-culture' (quoted in Frodon, 2000b: 32).

Statistical evidence shows that with only a minute budget at its disposal, EUROPA CINEMAS has managed to raise both the profile and the achievements of European films. In the network, the average programming percentage for European films is higher (63 per cent in 1999) than the minimum requirement (50 per cent) (see table 4.3).

Results and Criticisms of Eurimages

From the original twelve founding states, Eurimages membership has grown to twenty-six, a third of which now come from the former Eastern Bloc. Overall, between 1989 and 2000, Eurimages has supported the co-production of some 788 feature films and documentaries for a total of €214.3 million involving about 1,200 European producers (Eurimages Press Release, 2001).

While Eurimages has provided necessary support, criticisms of the programme identify its limitations. On average, Eurimages contributes 10 per cent of the budget for a co-production film.[9] As the cost of setting up international co-productions (e.g. transport and translation fees) can be as high as 10 per cent, critics of Eurimages argue that rather than a gain, the fund only compensates partners for engaging in co-production (Iordanova, 2002b; Wayne, 2002).[10] Some have even argued that it 'encourage[d] European producers to submit false, and in most cases, inflated budgets' (Finney, 1996: 110), an accusation strongly denied by Eurimages-supported producers. It has also been alleged that the fund gave French producers 'an unfair advantage in accessing funds' (p. 109) despite efforts to avoid any perception of French domination. Insiders are reported saying that the fund had 'highly tuned sensitivities to nationality' and even the composition of its staff was finely balanced to reflect different nationalities (*Screen Finance*, 2000c).

Eurimages was also criticised for its lack of success in film distribution. Although Eurimages-supported films received many distinctions and awards, this was not matched by greater cross-border appeal. An internal study carried out by Eurimages' Secretariat in 1996 showed that only 44.6 per cent of Eurimages-supported films had been released in all the countries of the three co-production partners. Over the period 1989–95, the majority of supported films (72.3 per cent) were released for a minimum of a week in the countries of their delegate producers, but this figure dropped to 40.4 per cent and 38 per cent respectively in the countries of the second and third party co-producers. Given the low-budget nature and cultural orientation of many of the films that received assistance from the fund, and considering the cultural aims of the fund, this criticism seems unfair.

OTHER SUPRANATIONAL FUNDS

Other initiatives regrouping countries with strong cultural affinities (IBERMEDIA) and/or geographical proximity (the Nordic Fund) were set up in the 1990s to promote and maintain the production and distribution of films and audiovisual programmes.

IBERMEDIA, an initiative of the Conference of Iberian–American Cinematographic Authorities (CICA), was approved in November 1997 at the summit of Iberian–American heads of state. It was 'directly inspired, in its philosophy, concept, objectives, operations and terms by the MEDIA and Eurimages programmes' (BIPE Conseil, 1998: 114–15). Spain, Mexico, Argentina, Brazil, Venezuela, Cuba, Portugal and Colombia all contributed to the programme.

The Nordic Film and Television Fund was formed in 1990 following an agreement between the Nordic Council and the national film institutes and broadcasters of Denmark, Finland, Iceland, Norway and Sweden. Initially reserved for the support of Nordic co-productions, the fund is now open to any projects on condition that the intended distribution involves at least two of the Nordic countries (p. 116). Like MEDIA and Eurimages, the Nordic Fund is now insisting on results, and has introduced more rigorous mechanisms for the recovery of its loans. As a result, production and distribution funding is allocated only to projects that can prove their market potential.

Table 4.4 Comparison of National and MEDIA Support

	(A) National Public Support 1995 (Ecu millions)	(B) MEDIA Support[1] (Ecu millions)	(B) / (A) (%)
Spain	27.3	6.4	23.4
UK	30.3	6.2	20.5
Italy	95.5	5.5	5.8
Germany	147.2	8.4	5.7
France	371.5	12.6	3.4
Total Five	**671.8**	**39.1**	**5.8**
Average Five	**134.4**	**7.8**	**5.8**
Ireland	3.8	1.8	46.8
Greece	5.2	1.5	29.7
Iceland	1.3	0.4	27.8
Belgium	23.8	4.3	18.0
Finland	11.5	1.6	13.5
Norway	14.8	1.6	10.9
Portugal	11.6	1.1	9.7
Netherlands	34.6	3.3	9.4
Sweden	25.7	2.2	8.5
Austria	21.9	1.7	7.9
Denmark	26.1	2.0	7.7
Luxembourg	1.5	0.1	7.7
Total Twelve	**181.8**	**21.6**	**11.9**
Average Twelve	**15.2**	**1.8**	**11.8**
Total Seventeen	853.6	60.7	7.1
Average Seventeen	50.2	3.6	7.2

Sources: BIPE Conseil (1998); MEDIA II Programme (1998: 104)

Note:
1. MEDIA support redistributed based on final beneficiaries, taking into account the automatic support for distribution generated, average 1996/97.

NATIONAL VERSUS EUROPEAN INITIATIVES

As table 4.4 indicates, MEDIA support can represent a substantial part of public support for Europe's film industries. MEDIA's contribution to public support varied between 3.4 per cent in France to as much as 46.8 per cent in Ireland. The programme is particularly beneficial for the smaller film-producing nations (e.g. Belgium, Greece and Iceland). With the British government still showing no intention of rejoining Eurimages, Scottish Screen negotiated to join the programme, believing that the membership fee of £200,000 a year was a small price to pay for access to the benefits of the fund and the capacity to entice European film-makers to work with Scottish partners in making English-language films. The considerable success of Danish films in the late 1990s and 2000 is often cited to illustrate the benefits of European support mechanisms for the smaller territories. Yet it must be pointed out that the Danish success rested on a very small number of well-marketed films. Not all the smaller film industries that received European support enjoyed the same success.

Despite the emphasis put by EU documents on the complementarity of MEDIA support and national systems, governments continue to set up their own initiatives to support their local industries, and bilateral arrangements are also flourishing. In the EU, nowhere is MEDIA support as important as national support. It is not surprising therefore to find that the view of many industry professionals today is that European support mechanisms are no substitute for government intervention.

Scrutiny of national regulations and other forms of local public support for films by DG IV, the EU department responsible for matters related to competition, has provoked anger. In October 2000, Jean Cazès, chairman of the European Producers Club (CPE), accused DG IV of 'totally distorting the agreement signed between the European Commission and France's CNC on public aid mechanisms to film' (quoted in Frodon, 2000a). The accusation came after the CPE had been informed by one of its members that in a document addressed to the Norwegian government, DG IV had enquired about the 'cultural nature' of Norwegian films and wanted to verify that they had received more than 50 per cent of public support. The CPE chairman called DG IV interference 'an ideological offensive' attacking the very principle of public support to the cultural industries. Voicing his anger, Cazès said: 'not only has the Commission been unable to create a European support mechanism for film and to help the coordination of existing national systems, but it is now trying to destroy what works well in each country'. He pointed out that *'Dancer in the Dark* would have never been possible if public aid mechanisms had been capped at 50 per cent' (quoted in Frodon, 2000a). To date, Brussels has approved all the national support mechanisms it has examined so far (Ireland, Denmark, France, the Netherlands, Germany and Sweden). It has been confirmed that European aid programmes will not be included in the 50 per cent restriction on public support to film.

The cultural remit of MEDIA and Eurimages may not have been abandoned, but attitudes and mentalities have changed within the industry and at national and European levels of government. A business-oriented approach is overtly encouraged by various new national film policies and by MEDIA Plus. Circulation potential is now a condition for funding from one of the new Eurimages schemes and distribution has to be secured. It is 'competitiveness, economic growth and employment issues' that Viviane Reding, the EU Commissioner for Education and Culture, stressed when she announced the MEDIA Plus budget in December 2000:

> [A €400 million budget] sends out a strong message to the audiovisual professionals that the fifteen Member States are fully behind the drive to increase the competitiveness of European cinema at a time when digital technology offers huge potential for growth and employment (*MEDIA France Bulletin*, 2000b).

However, this promotion of competitiveness would seem to be undermined by the European Commission's approval of mega-mergers increasing the power of the major global media corporations. In 2000, the Commission approved the merger of Canal Plus, Vivendi and Universal, as well as that of AOL with Time Warner, albeit, under certain conditions. Industry workers have expressed their concern that such a liberal attitude does little to contribute to the competitiveness of the European film industries and to safeguard employment.

CONCLUSION

In 1994, John Hill (1994: 67) argued that what had united the European film industries in the 1980s and early 90s was not a common identity but 'a shared situation and set of problems which certain forms of European collaboration [might] help alleviate'. There is little doubt the MEDIA and Eurimages initiatives have gone some way towards lessening the problems faced by the European film industries. At a time of intensified competition in the whole audiovisual sector, the contribution of these programmes to the industries of the smaller territories is particularly significant. The large number of applications to these programmes testifies to the importance of these funds.

While important, these programmes have not succeeded in developing a collective and competitive industrial logic to help the European film industries match the strength of Hollywood. When, in 1996, the trade publication *Screen International* launched polemics against the philosophy and operations of MEDIA, Jacques Delmoly (1996) wrote to say that 'if there [was] a synergy with national policies and professionals [were] mobilised, lasting structural effects could be achieved'. This view was challenged by Dieter Kosslick (1996), then president of the now-defunct MEDIA fund for distribution (EFDO), who claimed he had noted 'a detectable retreat behind national borders in the whole European media sector – with the UK taking the initiative with its exit from Eurimages'. Reflecting on what he perceived as the fading enthusiasm for a joint European film and media policy, Kosslick asserted:

The European audiovisual initiatives do not appear to have reached their goal of establishing a common audiovisual market. The euphoria has worn off, the sense of community is absent. There is only one person who could rally the creative forces and bureaucrats of the European film industry ... MPAA chief Jack Valenti. Valenti's insults to the European film industry during the GATT negotiations made the Europeans stand side-by-side in solidarity on a scale never seen before (p. 11).

MEDIA and Eurimages have now been operating for well over ten years. With the exception of the EUROPA CINEMAS network, a common film market is no more a reality today than it was at the inception of the programmes. A strong and effective pan-European distribution system still does not exist and the restructure of the film industries is far from complete. Europeans have not enthused over the European Film Academy Awards (Felix). That some of the more ambitious initiatives (e.g. the Multimedia Investment platform)[11] had to be halted shows how difficult it can be to replace the logic of association that prevailed in the mid-1990s with an industrial logic.

Moreover, important questions remain about the long-term direction and funding of MEDIA and Eurimages. There is a strong feeling among many industry professionals that the argument often heard today at EC and national levels concerning how public aid mechanisms may weaken the incentives of producers to make commercially attractive films, is used by public agencies to renounce cultural patronage. Caution is needed when assessing the faults and merits of MEDIA and Eurimages. Noting how the twenty-six-member Eurimages operates with the derisory annual budget of €21.4 million, Frédéric Sojcher (2000) warns of the dangers in 'continu[ing] to launch initiatives that pretend to compete with Hollywood hegemony' (author's translation) without giving them the means to achieve their objective. 'Could their relatively poor efficacy be used one day as an argument to do away with them altogether?' he asks. Talking of 'a double discourse', he wonders if setting up programmes such as 'MEDIA and Eurimages could not also become a way of having a good conscience on the cheap'.

Identifying the most effective mechanisms to build up and sustain the film industries of Europe is important. So are economic strategies to compete in the international market, but when 'cultural justifications for film policy are increasingly viewed as part of a wider competitiveness policy' (Pratten and Deakin, 2000: 222), the danger is that cultural priorities may disappear when there is no reason to retain a programme once it has managed to build a surplus budget.

NOTES

1. As Patrice Vivancos (2000: 80) notes, since MEDIA is regularly assessed at the end of a five-year period, it is much easier to criticise the MEDIA programme than other seemingly permanent existing support mechanisms.

2. The selective aid does not have to be repaid if the film generates low box-office takings. With a high rate of abandonment of debts (60 per cent in 1996 and 1997), selective support can constitute 'a virtually automatic form of support to distribution' (BIPE Conseil, 1998: 179) and appears to be better suited for the 'small distributors' in countries with a low volume of production.

3. *Breaking the Waves* alone generated 2.88 million admissions (that is, 83 per cent of admissions generated by Danish films in 1996).

4. This sum was cut back from the €500 million budget which had been ambitiously proposed by the European Parliament.

5. Figures supplied by Eurimages.

6. It has also been argued that those who engage in multilateral co-productions may often do so in order to access Eurimages funding.

7. In 1995, Eurimages supported ninety-nine co-productions (of which eighty-three were feature films and sixteen documentaries) and twenty-nine distributors.

8. Figures from Eurimages. At the time, the British government argued that the recently announced £80 million contribution to the UK film industry (until 2000) from National Lottery money would fill the gap left by the withdrawal from Eurimages. In 1997, the Labour government pledged to rejoin Eurimages but, to date, has not done so.

9. By 1998, the estimated budget of Eurimages-supported co-productions was some FF10 billion, to which Eurimages had contributed just below FF1.096 billion.

10. The author is grateful to both Dina Iordanova and Michael Wayne for advanced reading of the chapter/pages they were writing on European institutions (Iordanova, 2002b; Wayne, 2002).

11. The Multimedia Investment platform – created in 1996 to follow in the footsteps of the MEDIA Investment Club – ceased operating after MEDIA support was halted in 1997. Its aims were to develop the European multimedia industry with the support of major industrial groups, for the benefit of small and medium-sized companies, 'through the joint production of works with content using the new technologies' (BIPE Conseil, 1998: 73).

5

Film Distribution Networks within Europe

Distribution has always been important to success in the film industry. In this competitive age of global entertainment, marketing strategies play a decisive part in the success or failure of films in the international market. Distribution is central to the balance of power in the film business. The international distribution divisions of the major Hollywood studios dominate the distribution sector in Europe. Buena Vista International (the distribution arm of the Walt Disney Company), Columbia TriStar (the international division of Sony Pictures Entertainment), 20th Century-Fox (also handling MGM releases since November 2000), United International Pictures (UIP) (a joint venture between Paramount and Universal) and Warner Bros. form a concentrated core in Europe's distribution sector. European distributors have therefore had to struggle to find their place in the market alongside the majors.

Initially this chapter looks at the roles performed by distributors and sales agents, and explores the domination of European distribution by the Hollywood majors. Distributors have employed a range of established techniques to market and promote films and these are discussed alongside the new opportunities offered by online communications. Exploring particular territories, the chapter investigates how distribution is organised and structured in certain national contexts. During the 1990s, Europe's distribution sector witnessed a number of alliances between European distributors and the majors but also between distributors in the region. The chapter will finally consider to what extent large powerful groups can represent advantages or disadvantages for the distribution of European film.

DISTRIBUTION

Role of Distributors

A facilitator of product flow between producers and exhibitors, the distributor acquires distribution rights from producers and is responsible for selling and marketing a film. Typically, a distributor provides the producer with the services necessary to advertise, promote and generally market a picture. Distributors negotiate the release of films to cinemas and for each film they decide on the release pattern and the type of theatre booked. They plan the advertising and publicity campaigns for a film, organise the reproduction of prints, and may also arrange the licensing of the film to television companies, cable operators, video distributors and other outlets. A distributor collects revenues from the theatrical box office and other release windows and then pays these on to those parties holding a stake in the film.

Distributors also retain a significant role as film financiers. Distribution deals may take the form of either a minimum guarantee or negative pick-up. With the former, the distributor commits funds to the producer for specified distribution rights in advance of a film's release (Pham and Watson, 1993). This money can then contribute towards production and post-production costs. Negative pick-up occurs when a distributor (or international sales agent) acquires rights once a film is completed but without previously having had any involvement in production finance.

Film distribution is a high-risk business. Most films lose money on their theatrical run. Only a few enjoy substantial profits. The most successful distributors are therefore those with 'a sufficiently broad spread of films' to ensure that 'profits from a handful of pictures will outweigh any losses incurred by other films' (p. 84).

Sales Agents

In foreign territories, distributors frequently hire the services of a sales agent to act as their representative. The international sales community has traditionally been a small one with most of the leading international sales companies based in London or in the US (Pham and Watson, 1993: 32). Sales agents tend to conduct their business at a series of annual international film markets. Of the three major markets – the Cannes Film Festival, the American Film Market (AFM), and the Milan-based MIFED – only the last two are purely commercial markets where distributors discuss projects with agents, and films are advertised, viewed, bought and sold. Cannes tends to 'cross the perceived divide between the cultural and commercial sides of the industry: i.e. minority-audience "art-house" films and mass-market commercial productions' (Petrie, 1991: 118). As a result, 'particular films are targeted at particular markets depending on their form and content' (*ibid.*). Other festivals (Berlin, Karlovy Vary, Locarno, London, Rotterdam, Sundance, Toronto, Venice, etc.) can also act as a marketplace for European films.

US Dominance of European Markets

During 2000, US films took 73 per cent of the European market (70 per cent in 1999) and 93.3 per cent (92.1 per cent in 1999) in their home market (EAO,

2001a). In return, European films accounted for only 3.9 per cent of admissions at the North American box office that year (3.6 per cent in 1999). Considering how the competitive positions of the US and European film industries worldwide are 'significantly affected by the respective structures of the distribution functions', Coopers & Lybrand (1993: 12) have identified the following features as accounting for the dominance of the major US studio distributors:

- overheads of the distribution process are spread over a large number of films
- the distributor's profit margin is ultimately owned by the studio and thus contributes to the overall income earned by the producers
- the large volume of advertising spend undertaken by the major distributors results in considerable leverage over the pricing of advertising space in the various media
- similarly, the large volume of releases results in considerable bargaining power over the exhibitors, possibly resulting in preferential release dates and terms of trade
- audience information can be gathered for a wide portfolio of films which can be fed to the studios for consideration in developing future commercially oriented product
- a worldwide distribution network providing knowledge and insights for all significant territories
- direct access to the world markets through their overseas offices and versatility in releasing films to theatrical markets around the world

In addition, the huge size of the English-language market constitutes an enormous advantage for US distributors.

Unlike most European distributors, the marketing and distribution arms of the Hollywood majors are already involved with a film's production at the development stage. This process can sometimes involve consultation with the overseas distribution arms of the studios.

Traditionally, the majors have handled very few European non-English-language films. As noted in the report, *Retailing European Films*, prepared by London Economics (1993) for the MEDIA Business School, 'US distributors will distribute films from other countries, but they expect them to exceed the average performance of US films'. The report observed 'US distributors may well be biased towards US product ... because they need a higher return on EC product to achieve the same margin as on their own product' (p. 100).

DISTRIBUTION STRATEGIES
Marketing and Promotional Techniques
Film distribution uses a number of well-established techniques to market and promote films:

- marketing: posters, press, television and radio advertising, theatrical trailers, websites
- promotions: screenings/previews, publicising box-office performance or festival and other awards won, exploiting controversy, star and director appearances, merchandising, press and television campaigns or competitions, and use of subsidiary devices (paperback edition of the screenplay, soundtrack records)
- PR: targeting of opinion-formers, such as critics, journalists, broadcasters, fan clubs

Posters remain important for film advertising. A visual medium par excellence, posters often need to be adapted to local sensitivities. While countries such as France and the Netherlands are more liberally minded as far as the display of sexuality is concerned, Britain and Italy tend to show a more conservative approach.

The aggressive promotion of film has not gone unopposed in Europe. For example in France, where film is also considered an art form, emphasis on marketability and profitability has long been anathema to many film professionals, who have viewed the application of marketing tools and techniques to cinema with suspicion. Laurent Creton even talked of the incompatibility between marketing and cinema as first and foremost an ideological problem: 'To talk about film as a mere product triggers violent reactions. [. . .] Marketing and the even more derogatory term "commercialisation" suggest the American model of capital and power, and of a supermarket civilisation' (author's translation, 1994: 123). When the issue of 'cultural exception' dominated the GATT talks in 1993, Jacques Toubon, the French Minister of Culture, used the example of the 450-print release of *Jurassic Park* (Steven Spielberg 1993 US) to denounce American distribution and promotion practices and criticise the role of UIP in Europe.

While massive releases and marketing deals with mass-consumed product chains such as McDonald's restaurants continue to reinforce fears of American cultural hegemony, attitudes are changing. Following the practice of the US majors' international offices, European distributors are now fully engaged in similar large-scale promotional deals. Even in France, policy-makers, producers and distributors are now prepared to acknowledge the importance of marketing strategies. As Creton points out (1997), marketing is 'a precious tool to launch a film' and increasingly has a role in 'defin[ing] a project' (author's translation, p. 159).

With international box-office revenues now exceeding US revenues for the Hollywood majors, the international marketing departments of the majors are assuming a certain degree of autonomy in planning local marketing campaigns. Even though some of the sequences used in trailers may be the same in Europe as in America, the marketing campaigns are often tailored to local conditions. Changes are usually motivated by cultural attitudes and/or media conditions (Hazelton, 1996).

Today, merchandising and promotional tie-ins are no longer the prerogative of US companies, even if the latter continue to be the main practitioners of these strategies. European companies involved in tie-ins tend to 'prefer the guarantee of Hollywood distribution efficiency to the unknown potential of a smaller local distributor' (Stafford, 1999: 11). In the UK, for instance, Buena Vista International joined up with British Telecom to promote *102 Dalmatians* (issuing special phone cards), while Paramount Pictures and Volvo launched a worldwide campaign to cross-promote *The Saint* (Phillip Noyce 1997 US) and Volvo's new C70 coupé. In France, promotion of *The Net* (Irwin Winkler 1995 US) involved joint marketing efforts between Columbia TriStar, Apple, Hachette-Multimédia and French radio station Europe 2. The latter disrupted its programmes with 'live terrorist informations' mimicking the film's plot.

French distribution companies and advertising agencies have worked with fashion, food, liqueur, perfume and car manufacturers, banks and tourist agencies in joint marketing efforts to launch films. The French release of *1492, Conquest of Paradise*, Ridley Scott's film celebrating the 500th anniversary of Columbus's journey to America, and starring Gérard Depardieu, coincided with the launch of a new perfume range called Christopher Columbus. The film also had the support of a French bank, Crédit Agricole, which launched a promotion campaign in its 2,500 branches all over the country.

Marketing strategies often emphasise the perceived strengths of a particular country. In Russia, the marketing during 1999 of Nikita Mikhalkov's *Sibirskij Tsiryulnik* (*The Barber of Siberia*) aimed 'to show the world what a beautiful country Russia is' (Beumers, 2000: 205). The campaign included the positioning of banners and posters all over Moscow, together with the launch of a new brand of vodka (Russian Standard) and a new perfume range (Cadet No. 1 and Cadet No. 3). *Sibirskij Tsiryulnik* was premiered at the Kremlin Palace of Congress, the first time since 1974 that the 5,000-seat venue had been used for a screening.

Television advertising is regarded as one of the most effective forms of marketing because it reaches 'a mass audience instantaneously with major impact from carefully designed trailer sequences' (Stafford, 1999: 10). However, the high cost of advertising on television is usually beyond the budget of small independent distributors. In several territories, including France, television advertising is banned for fear that Hollywood films would enjoy a much greater promotion and so increase American supremacy. This may soon change. In any case, such legislation has not prevented public and private channels from showing clips.

In Europe, stars and directors are now often drawn into tours intended to display the production credentials of a film and build audience awareness. Many European actors and actresses increasingly participate in publicity campaigns. This is not always specified in actors' contracts and there have been several instances where promotional activities have backfired. Sophie Marceau and Gérard Depardieu, for example, have used their international star status to criticise the films they had just made and the system that helped making them. Marceau publicly criticised *Marquise* (Véra Belmont 1997 France/Italy/Switzerland/Spain), a film in which she played the title role and, in 2000, Depardieu accused French producers of using French financing to 'line their pockets', making films with little appeal to audiences (Neumann, 2000).

Press criticism continues to perform a vital function in defining public opinion about films. However, coverage by the European press can often marginalise European films. As Stafford (1999: 9) points out with reference to the British context, European films are 'being relegated to the last and smallest review position in the newspaper, often despite the film critic's enthusiasm [as] the papers are looking to ensure a wider circulation by prioritising more "popular" films'. The wide press coverage given to European cinema in French daily papers such as *Le Monde* or *Libération* is probably unique.

There is also a common perception among distributors of challenging films that critics often prevent audiences from making up their own mind about such films, and in the last few years, critics have been taken to task by the industry.[1] Distributors can take extreme action to make sure films are seen regardless of critics' opinions. 'Bad reviews are the last thing you'd expect a film distributor to draw attention to when trying to win audiences for a radically different movie,' wrote Nick James (2000: 3), the editor of *Sight and Sound*. Yet this is exactly what FilmFour did when publicising *Dancer in the Dark* in the UK. Angry and frustrated by 'the mauling Lars von Trier's musical received from several broadsheet critics' (p. 3), FilmFour pledged to refund the cost of admission to anyone who walked out in the first hour. Needless to say distributors rarely go to such extremes.

CASE STUDY: TRANSLATING FILM TITLES

Film titles are central tools in marketing campaigns. When marketing films between European territories, word-for-word translation of a title rarely works.

Marketing executive Lisa Heyes partly blamed the UK failure of *Le Huitième jour* (1996 Belgium/France/UK) – Jaco van Dormael's award-winning film about the friendship between an estranged husband (Daniel Auteuil) and a man with Down's Syndrome – on its English title:

> This was a brilliant film but essentially it was an art house film, which could have crossed over. However, by calling it *The Eighth Day* instead of its original French title, *Le Huitième jour*, and cutting a trailer with an English voiceover, it sounded like a poor man's *Rain Man*. The result was that art house audiences said it wasn't for them and mainstream audiences said it wasn't for them either (quoted in Bateman 1999: 13).

International distributors need to exercise a little creative thinking when it comes to adapting titles for different markets, as the case of *Gazon maudit* (Josiane Balasko 1995 France) illustrates. The film is a comedy about the disrupting effect which the arrival of a lesbian has on the life of a chauvinist male-dominated couple. The film's title is a pun that works on many levels in French, but it is also an old slang term referring to pubic hair. In Spanish, a direct translation (*Felpudo Maldito*) has the same connotation as the French expression – a type of grass that men must keep off. In Italy, the title was translated as 'Shame it Had to be a Woman' and in Germany, it became 'One Woman for Two'. Patrick Frater and Ana Maria Bahiana (1996: 25) reported that, in anglo-

Le Huitième jour (*The Eighth Day*, 1996)

phone territories, 'Balasco was understood to have insisted at one stage that the English-language title should include the word "lesbian", a recipe for certain death in the US, but Miramax came up with the more ambiguous *French Twist*, also to be used for the UK.' The strategy worked well, for *Gazon maudit* was one of the most successful French-language exports of the mid-1990s.

Festivals and Markets

Festivals provide a context for the distribution of films outside the conventional parameters of commercial exhibition. About 1,000 festival venues (Vivancos, 2000: 108) are located within the wider Europe, 800 of which are in the European Union (attracting around 8 million admissions, 12 per cent of cinema audiences). This represents the equivalent of a parallel distribution circuit. However, showing films at festivals involves certain risks for small distributors. For the few films that come away with a prize or buyers, there are many that are killed 'with unkind reviews' (Ryan, 1995: 14). In addition, some festivals are difficult to get into or require an entry fee.[2]

Regional, national or European levels of public support exist to assist with both organisation and attendance of participants at domestic and international film festivals. MEDIA support for some of these events consists of a direct grant to festivals as well as support for co-ordination between festivals (to qualify, 62 per cent of a festival's films must originate from at least five different European countries). Early support has borne fruit. For the whole of the European Union, between 1992 and 1995, the share of European films in the MEDIA-supported festivals increased by 30 per cent. Since then, European programmes have committed to develop synergies between festivals and the distribution sector.

Internet Marketing

Europeans are increasingly choosing to promote their films on the web. Internet sites have a number of advantages as a marketing tool. Mark Morris (2000) lists these as:

- the cheapness of the web compared to billboard, magazine or press ads
- sites have greater durability than conventional advertising (they often go live months before a film's release but can still remain active for a video/DVD release)
- sites provide discussion forums that allow audiences to feel more involved with a film than other forms of marketing
- the capacity to address teenagers and young adults, the Internet's main users, who form the main core of the filmgoing audience

- sites provide market-research intelligence by tracking the number of hits for a site
- sites offer low-budget productions a useful replacement for print ads

In their efforts to build early audience interest, several European film companies have set up websites inviting web surfers to watch casting sessions, rushes online, and to get involved with a film's screenplay, researching characters and voting on plot twists. Employed in 1998 to promote the film *La Patinoire* (*The Ice Rink*) (Jean-Philippe Toussaint 1998 Belgium/France/Italy/Germany), this method of drawing in the audience was regarded as giving regular visitors 'a sense of having a stake in the success of the film' (Morris, 2000: 14). It also changes the way films are conceived.

With the use of the Internet as a marketing channel, the film industry has become further integrated into the commercial cultural economy which for so long has benefited Hollywood over European cinema:

> Net users are now accustomed to free-to-access sites, which makes Web publishers solely reliant on advertising revenue. This in turn favours the growth of general-interest sites generating a viable amount of visitor traffic for advertisers, which, in the case of film-related sites, leads to a concentration on commercial Hollywood cinema. Sound familiar? (Stables, 1999: 4).

It seems certain that the Internet will play a greater role in film marketing in the future. However, uncertainty remains over how useful this channel of promotion will be. In the past, distributors and exhibitors claimed they knew some films worked better with specific audiences than others and that certain marketing techniques worked better in particular territories than in others. No such certainty exists today. Research shows that the 'youth segment's growing immunity to old-fashioned marketing presents something of a headache' to the marketing experts employed by the large distribution groups (Brown, 2000).

Promotion Costs

Marketing budgets, like film budgets, have soared in the last decade. In France, investment in film advertising grew by 50 per cent between 1995 and 1999 (*CNC Info*, 2001a). The inflation of marketing costs is linked in a vicious circle with rising production costs. To recover inflated production costs, a mass audience must be found, and to create that audience requires a giant publicity budget. However, the more successful a film is in the cinemas, the more distributors can charge later for ancillary rights, which include everything from television to other non-theatrical outlets such as army bases, prisons, airlines and car-ferries. Competition is intense and the large European players are now mounting huge publicity campaigns (with matching budgets) to build up audience anticipation.

In 1993, Coopers & Lybrand noted that 'marketing expenditure on feature films had outgrown consumer expenditure in most territories' (p. 35). They estimated that spending was 'too high' and that increased sophistication in marketing techniques and greater competition was responsible for such 'disproportionate growth'. The spread of multiplexes across Europe and an ever-increasing number of prints for the more commercial fare have only contributed to reinforce this inflationary trend. At a time when the theatrical life of a film is made shorter by the development of ancillary markets, a film is expected to achieve higher admissions in a smaller number of weeks.

It is difficult to estimate the degree to which marketing expenditure correlates with subsequent box-office performance but, if one looks at the most successful European films of the last decade, there is little doubt that marketing strategies have played a significant part in their achievements at the box office. The extraordinary box-office success of *Four Weddings and a Funeral* (US$350 million worldwide gross) was hailed as a watershed in British cinema, but owed much to the huge promotion efforts of its distributor, PolyGram. Made on a US$3.5 million budget, *The Full Monty* took US$205 million worldwide in 1997. Its American distributor, Fox Searchlight, was reported to have spent over ten times the film's budget on its international marketing. In the UK, where the film took US$69 million, Fox Searchlight positioned it as 'a must see' film that had already done great business in America (Bateman, 1999: 13). Lisa Heyes, head of UK marketing at FilmFour, and former marketing executive at PolyGram during the release of the low-budget British hit *Trainspotting*, believed that targeting an audience was crucial for low-budget films. In the case of *Trainspotting*, the target audience was the young cinemagoing audience, and the UK marketing spend was £1 million, half the film's budget. In a similar move, in 1999 FilmFour was reported to have 'earmarked £1 million for the £2.5 million comedy *East is East* despite the fact that there was no recognisable talent attached to the film' (p. 13).

British films and other European English-language films are certainly easier to sell than foreign-language films. When the French comedy, *Mon père, ce héros* (Gérard Lauzier 1991), starring Gérard Depardieu, was released in Germany, it achieved a satisfactory 300,000 admissions. Eighteen months later and with a bigger marketing push, *My Father the Hero* (Steve Miner 1994), the US scene-for-scene remake featuring the same lead, notched up more than 850,000 admissions. As Patrick Frater (1996) comments, the example 'is particularly pertinent as the divergence cannot be explained by star power; and the same actor dubbed Depardieu into German in both versions' (p. 15). Reflecting on the fact that *My Father the Hero* was also more successful in Spain where both the original French version and the American remake were dubbed, one French industry analyst wondered whether, rather than being a question of marketing power and access to screens, French films did not suffer from a 'negative a-priori assumption' outside their home territory (Boudier, 1994: 4).

Table 5.1 Box-Office Revenue of European Foreign-language Films on Release in the United States (1999)

Film	Distributor	Release Date	Maximum Number of Screens	Cumulative Box Office US$	Screen Average US$
Life is Beautiful (Italy)	Miramax	23/10/98	1,136	57,247,384	50,394
All About My Mother (Spain/France)	Sony Classics	19/11/99	145	8,012,562	55,259
Run Lola Run (Germany)	Sony Classics	18/6/99	172	7,276,585	42,253
Jakob the Liar (Germany/US)	Sony	24/9/99	1,200	4,956,401	4,130
Autumn Tale (France)	October	9/7/99	50	2,084,347	41,687
The Dream Life of Angels (France)	Sony Classics	2/4/99	64	1,726,567	26,978
The Celebration (Denmark)	October	9/10/98	36	1,656,223	46,006
Romance (France)	Trimark/ Odeon	17/9/99	54	1,314,053	24,334
The Castle (Austria)	Miramax	7/5/99	56	877,621	15,672
Lovers of the Arctic Circle (Spain/France)	New Line	9/4/99	23	507,532	22,067
Lucie Aubrac (France)	USA Films	17/9/99	18	461,268	25,626
Open Your Eyes (Spain/France/Italy)	Artisan	16/4/99	34	370,720	10,904
Bicycle Thieves (Italy)	Kino	2/10/98	5	334,293	66,859
The Grandfather (Spain)	Miramax	8/10/99	12	54,468	4,539

Sources: *Screen Finance* (2000a: 5)

Distribution of European Films Outside Europe

In the 1970s and 80s, the American market became less receptive to foreign films as a whole than at any time since the Second World War (Waterman and Jayakar, 2000: 502). This situation did not improve in the 1990s, however 1999 has been considered a possible turning point for the fate of European films in foreign markets, particularly in the US. That year, European films and co-productions made a greater impact than in previous years, taking 5.41 per cent of the total US box office (compared to 1.47 per cent in 1998). Growth was attributable to the success of UK films such as *Notting Hill* (Roger Michell 1999 UK/US), *The World is Not Enough* and the English-language French film *Joan of Arc*. The most successful foreign-language European films were *La vita è bella* (*Life is Beautiful*), *Todo sobre mi madre* (*All About My Mother*) and *Lola Rennt* (*Run Lola Run*) (Drinnan, 2000) (see table 5.1). Although produced or part-produced by European film-makers, these films were distributed in the US by divisions of the Hollywood majors.

For French films, 1997 was the first year that foreign admissions (56 million, 13 million of which were for French-language films) exceeded domestic admissions (51 million). However, the English-language production, *The Fifth Element*, accounted for approximately two-thirds of foreign admissions that year. France has since intensified promotion of its films abroad. Fifteen French films and thirteen French co-productions appeared on cinema screens in North America in the first half of 2000, more than in the whole of 1999. Other initiatives by Unifrance have focused on under-exploited territories in South America and South East Asia.

In Europe, a number of bilateral schemes appeared in the late 1990s to ensure that national films received distribution in the European Union. Among these were the creation of a Franco-German Film Academy and Chancellor Schröder's proposal for Franco-German co-operation in distribution, a strategy similar to a French–Italian scheme already in existence. In 2000, a programme of twinned British and French activities was launched. Called 'A French Connection' in the UK and 'Typiquement British' in France, the programme was supported in the UK by the British Council and the British Film Institute, and the Centre Georges Pompidou in France. Screening over 200 features, a five-month festival of British films (2000–2001) opened in Paris with a tribute to the Redgrave family and offered French audiences a wide range of recent and old films, including strands on France as viewed by British film-makers, and London from the 1960s to the 90s. In exchange, UK audiences were given the opportunity to enjoy a taste of French film which included a retrospective of Jean-Luc Godard at the National Film Theatre in London and a video release from the British Film Institute for a number of classic titles of French cinema. It remains to be seen how far these bilateral initiatives will continue to be supported.

FILM DISTRIBUTION IN LEADING TERRITORIES

Despite the trend towards concentration and internationalisation, the European distribution market remains fragmented and volatile. In the majority of territories, the number of active distributors has only slightly increased (see table 5.2) between 1995 and 1999, the most significant growth being between 1995 and 1997 (*Screen Digest*, 2000c: 187). However, despite the efforts of the MEDIA programme to strengthen the sector, European distribution remains divided along linguistic lines in multilingual countries such as Belgium, Luxembourg and Switzerland and national lines (releases and release patterns still vary from one country to another). As a closer examination of recent trends in several European countries illustrates, the situation is far from uniform and remains subject to rapid changes.

Germany

In Germany, the distribution sector was said to have 'experienced a shakeout following the public flotations of 1998 and 1999 which injected millions of Deutschmarks into such distribution outfits as Kinowelt, Senator Film, Constantin Film, Helkon Media, Advanced Medien and Highlight' (*Screen International*, 2000: 44). These distributors were involved in risky bidding wars to obtain licences to attractive feature films, particularly American ones. In 2000, Jeff Colvin of Imperial Entertainment Bank was quoted in *Screen International* as saying that German buyers had 'stepped up to become the driving force for large US productions':

Table 5.2 Number of Active Distributors in the EU (1996–9)

	1996	1997	1998	1999
Belgium	30	33	27	25
Denmark	22	22	21	18
Finland	8	22	20	20
France	163	156	161	158
Germany	45	51	53	59
Ireland	6	8	8	8
Italy	23	26	28	27
Luxembourg	1	1	1	
Netherlands	25	22		
Portugal	13	15	15	15
Spain	42	45	48	51
Sweden	16	16	19	25
UK	54	49	51	52
Total EU	465	483	471	478

Source: *Screen Digest* (2000c: 187)

Table 5.3 Leading Distributors in Germany (1999)

Distributor	Films	Market Share (%)[1]	Most Successful Release
UIP	28	18.66	*The Mummy*
BVI	34	17.77	*Just Married*
Fox	18	12.48	*Star Wars I – The Phantom Menace*
Warner Bros.	17	12.32	*The Matrix*
Kinowelt	41	11.29	*Rush Hour*
Constantin	11	5.82	*Astérix und Obélix*
Columbia TriStar	17	5.73	*Big Daddy*
Universal	17	5.27	*Notting Hill*
Senator	12	2.84	*Aimée und Jaguar*
Tobis	8	1.79	*Message in a Bottle*
Delphi	3	1.55	*Sonnenallee*
Concorde	15	1.06	*The 13th Warrior*
Others	114	3.35	
Total	335	100.00	

Source: Vital (2000b)

Note:
1. According to number of admissions.

the producer or the sales agent will come to our office and invariably has the German sale, and they will have that for a nice chunk of the budget. That has been the easiest sale for them to get and the most lucrative. Sometimes, it was even as large as the US sale (p. 44).

While several smaller distribution companies have been taken over by larger groups, new entrants have also arrived, and the number of active distributors has risen slightly (59 per cent in 1999 compared with 53 per cent the previous year). This does not necessarily mean a better deal for German or other European films. In 1999, 85 per cent of the films acquired by German distribution companies were American. Among Germany's leading distributors (see table 5.3), only two companies (Constantin and Senator) concentrated their efforts on domestic productions. If German distributors managed to capture a 28 per cent share of the market that year, it was largely due to the performance of their English-language films.

The UK

Reporting on the situation of independent distributors in Britain during the late 1990s, Eddie Dyja (1999: 41) found that the market was extremely fragmented,

Table 5.4 Leading Distributors in the UK (1999)

Distributor	Films	Market Share (%)	Most Successful Release
UIP	46	23.5	*Notting Hill*
Buena Vista	33	22.1	*A Bug's Life*
Fox	24	14.4	*Star Wars I – The Phantom Menace*
Warner Bros.	23	11.52	*The Matrix*
UPI	17	8.24	*Mickey Blue Eyes*
Entertainment	26	6.26	*Austin Powers: The Spy Who Shagged Me*
Columbia TriStar	25	5.78	*Big Daddy*
Pathé	12	3.56	*The Blair Witch Project*
FilmFour	21	2.7	*East is East*
Artificial Eye	15	0.2	*Place Vendôme*
Metrodome	13	0.46	*Human Traffic*
Alliance	14	0.4	*eXistenZ*
Downtown Pictures	12		*Orphans*
BFI	12		*Get Carter*
Blue Dolphin	5		
Metro Tartan	6		
Gala	6		
ICA	9		
Others	41		
Total	360		

Sources: Data compiled from *Screen Finance*, 2000b: 8 and 2000d: 7
Note: Market share expressed as percentage of total box office.

with 45 per cent of distribution companies releasing only one film. Distribution in the UK has long been in the hands of the US majors. As a result, the profits of successful films such as *The Full Monty* and *Notting Hill* have gone to America.

Even though films involving UK producers more than doubled their domestic box-office gross in 1999 (up from £42.9 million in 1998 to £104 million), the Hollywood majors continued to increase their hold on the UK market, releasing 168 films that year compared with 134 in 1998 (see table 5.4).[3] After the closure of First Independent in 1997 and the takeover of PolyGram by Seagram in 1998, the majors held an even larger share of the total UK box office (85.5 per cent in 1999 compared with 82.4 per cent in 1998) (*Screen Finance*, 2000b: 6). Of the independents, Pathé has become the most important distributor of UK films in 2000, overtaking FilmFour, which had traditionally stood as the company most willing and able to promote British pictures. Pathé's rise to success in 2000 (ranking fifth behind the majors) was largely due to one film, *Chicken Run*, the Aardman Animation/DreamWorks SKG picture, which represented 65 per cent of the distributor's market share.

Roy Stafford (1999: 8) reported that during the 1990s, 'there had been a nar-rowing . . . of the range of films in distribution' following the closure of a number of small UK-owned distribution companies. He also pointed out that the situation had become worse for foreign-language pictures in Britain:

> the ghettoisation of foreign language films in television graveyard slots has meant that broadcasters are buying fewer of these films and paying less for them. This had an impact upon distributors already struggling to justify purchase prices in a territory that has some of the lowest returns for foreign language film in all of Europe. Everyone cites the fact that the audience for this kind of films is dwindling, but as lower income leads to less films in distribution, this could be seen as a self-fulfilling prophesy (p. 9).

During 2000, the UK saw a marked increase in the annual number of films released, but European non-English-language films continue to fare poorly at the box office despite the rise of Pathé and the efforts of the smaller British independent distributors.

France

Domestic distributors hold a stronger position in France than in Germany or the UK. Investing heavily in both French film production and distribution, the oli-gopoly of Gaumont, Pathé and UGC has played an important role in the promotion of French cinema.[4] In 1999 the top three distributors (GBVI, Pathé and UFD) controlled 39.47 per cent of the market (see table 5.5). That year, while Pathé released nineteen French films (including five French co-produc-tions) and only three American films, of the twenty-three films released by UFD, seventeen were American, and of GBVI's eighteen new releases, thirteen were American titles, one Australian and only four were French films (including Besson's English-language *Joan of Arc*). Bac Films – now owned by Studio Canal – slightly increased its number of American releases from thirteen films in 1998 (out of twenty-five films) to fourteen in 1999 (out of twenty-four new releases). When, in 2000, Bac Distribution became the third most important distributor in France, it was largely due to the success of its four best-performing films, which were all American.

As in other countries, the trend has been for a small number of distributors (including the US majors) to take a large slice of the French box office. In 1999, the top ten distributors captured 86.1 per cent of admissions in France (85.5 per cent in 2000). The remainder of the market was made up of small com-panies, many of which handled only one title a year. For these companies, a single failure can have catastrophic consequences, as illustrated by the collapse

Table 5.5 Leading Distributors in France (1999)

Distributor	Films	Market Share (%)[1]	Most Successful Release
GBVI	18	14.01	*Tarzan*
Pathé Distribution	24	12.85	*Astérix et Obélix*
UFD	23	12.61	*Star Wars 1 – The Phantom Menace*
UIP	31	11.73	*The Mummy*
Warner Bros.	17	10.91	*The Matrix*
Bac Films	24	7.98	*Quasimodo d'el Paris*
Columbia TriStar	30	4.83	*Sex Intentions*
Universal Pictures	18	4.78	*Notting Hill*
Metropolitan	22	4.68	*Rush Hour*
Pyramide	11	1.77	*Vénus Beauté*
Mars Films	22	1.73	*The Blair Witch Project*
Ocean Films	13	1.72	*Le ciel, les oiseaux et ... ta mère*
SND	10	1.13	*Mon père, ma mère, mes frères*
MK2 Diffusion	13	1.01	*Au coeur du mensonge*
ARP Selection	10	1.00	*Rosetta*
Rezo Films	9	0.90	*Rien sur Robert*
Gebeka	3	0.85	*Babar, roi des éléphants*
Diaphana	9	0.77	*C'est quoi la vie?*
Opening Distribution	10	0.73	*Chucky's fiancée*
Gemini Films	8	0.72	*La nouvelle Eve*
Films du Losange	5	0.56	*Adieu, plancher des vaches*
CTV International	6	0.33	*Beowulf*
Goutte d'Or Distrib.	3	0.32	*La dilettante*
Eurozoom	7	0.17	*Babar, roi des éléphants*
Cinema Public Films	11	0.16	*The New Adventures of Munk and Lenny*
Others	238	1.75	
Total	595	100	

Source: *Le Film français* (2000a: 37)

Note:
1. According to number of admissions.

of Amorces Diffusion in 1995. With Amorces, French independent Richard Magnien had carved out a small but distinctive niche in the distribution of art-house pictures, but his company was sunk by the failure of just one film, *O Covento* (Mañoel de Oliveira 1995 Portugal/France). In competition at Cannes and boasting an international cast led by John Malkovich and Catherine Deneuve, *O Covento* was released in September 1995. By the end of the year, the film had made only 53,000 admissions in France (26,898 in Paris, after a fifteen-week run) (*Le Film français*, 1996: 37). Asserting that *O Covento* was 'just the kind of film that ought to be made available to cinemagoers around Europe', a British industry analyst speculated that 'the asking price was probably unrealistically high' (*Sight and Sound*, 1996: 5).

The fate of Amorces Diffusion illustrates the fragile situation of small distributors, even in a country such as France where distributors, along with producers and exhibitors, benefit from various state aids. While France's automatic aid generally tends to better serve the distribution arms of the French conglomerates backing the more commercial films, selective aids are more generously awarded to independent companies. French selective aids reflect the CNC's wish to maintain equilibrium between the larger groups and the small or medium-sized distribution companies. Selective aids to film distribution have different aims: help is provided to launch French and foreign films which involve a certain risk, or to support distributors of *art et essai* films, while in other cases aid is offered to distributors of films originating from countries whose films are little known in France.[5] In addition, France's film export body, Unifrance, plays a major part in the distribution and exhibition of French films worldwide.

Other European Territories

France is not the only EU country to have adopted measures at a national level to support film distribution. However, only Spain operated screen quotas in the late 1990s. Quotas were abolished in 2000, but in 2001, industry pressure led the Spanish government to reinstate them, for the following five years at least. The quota system – supported by producers – required exhibitors to programme no less than one day of European film for every three days spent showing non-European films.

Portuguese distribution is highly concentrated. In 1999, the five major companies released 90.5 per cent of the titles. With the exception of Atalanta Filmes, which released many films of EU origin (59.4 per cent of the company's titles), the catalogues of the main companies were almost exclusively US films (Taborda, 2001: 3).

Italy's support scheme helps the distribution of domestic films, both at home and abroad, and includes selective aid to assist the distribution of a few prestigious European films, usually auteur films. In the last decade, Italian selective aid has supported the distribution of, among others, the films of: Alain Resnais, *On connaît la chanson* (*Same Old Song*) (1997 France/Switzerland/UK/Italy); Carlos Saura, *Tango* (1998 Spain/Argentina/France/Germany); Pavel Chukhrai, *Vor* (*The Thief*) (1997 France/Russia); and Aleksandr Sokurov, *Mat i syn* (*Mother and Son*) (1997 Germany/Russia).

The Film Centre in Greece subsidises the distribution of films produced within the framework of its so-called Horizons II programme (introduced in 1998). Films are assessed on a case-by-case basis and it is required that producers already have an agreement with a distribution company. In the Netherlands, the national government supports the distribution of 'non-commercial films of artistic merit'. Within the framework of the 1997–2000 Cultural Policy Document, the Ministry of Education, Culture and Science subsidised three 'non-commercial distributors': Cinemien, the Netherlands Film Museum/ International Art Film, and Contact Film Cinematheek.

Denmark's distribution business is dominated by the country's leading entertainment groups, Nordisk Film and Metronome. In existence since 1906, Nordisk is one of the oldest film production companies in the world. Today, Nordisk Film Biografdistribution, and its independent distribution arm, Constantin Film, have long-term contracts with Columbia TriStar and 20th Century-Fox. Metronome has an alliance with Warner to handle the studio's films locally. Buena Vista International and UIP operate their own divisions. While new distributors have emerged, the number of independent and arthouse distributors has been declining. The Danish Film Institute (DFI) operates several schemes to support the promotion of feature films. Promotion and print subsidies go to Danish films that have already benefited from selective aid for production. The DFI pays 50 per cent of the price of prints, and supports as many as seventy-five prints for local films. Another scheme assists the import of quality films and helps to finance prints of foreign films with artistic value. The DFI also supports the marketing of local films, both at home and abroad.[6]

MERGERS AND ALLIANCES IN EUROPEAN DISTRIBUTION
Alliances in the 1990s
Over the last decade, the limited growth potential of the US market led the majors to seek to strengthen their positions in European distribution markets through mergers and alliances. These corporate manoeuvrings were aimed at maximising revenues and exploiting the latest technological advances in distribution.

While the majors are US-based, this should not obscure the fact that these companies have now grown to become large pan-regional companies, managing distribution through networks of offices in key national markets. 20th Century-Fox, for instance, now has joint venture deals with Warner and Sony in Europe, together with local partners in France (UGC) and Spain (Hispano Foxfilm).[7] European distribution groups have formed alliances with the majors, including GBVI, Gaumont's partnership with Buena Vista International, and UGC with Fox (UFD) in France, Mediaset with Castle Rock Entertainment, BIM with Columbia in Italy, and in Spain, Lauren Films with Buena Vista and Sogecine with Warner Bros.[8] In the late 1990s, some of the most important independent distributors were also seeking deals with American distributors. In Germany, all major production and distribution companies have forged alliances and/or signed deals with American or other European companies, for example Kinow-elt's venture with the Canadian company Alliance Releasing, called Momentum Pictures, for distribution in the UK.

After the failure of the Eurotrustees venture (see Chapter 1), other attempts were made to build a European distribution network to rival the power of the Hollywood majors. These included the efforts of PolyGram and Kinowelt (see below), and the two French companies, Ciby Sales – parent company of Ciby 2000 – and Pathé. By 1997, Pathé owned UK distributor Guild – renamed Pathé Distribution – AMLF in France and had a stake in Germany's Tobis Filmkunkst.

CASE STUDY: POLYGRAM FILMED ENTERTAINMENT

Before the 1998 takeover by the Canadian drinks company Seagram, and its subsequent absorption into Vivendi Universal, PolyGram was often regarded as a viable contender to form a pan-European distribution outfit. PolyGram Filmed Entertainment (PFE) emerged from the PolyGram Music Video operation set up in the early 1980s. Already one of the world's major recorded music companies, PolyGram was majority-owned by the Dutch electronics giant Philips, a rich parent able to support the company's diversification into film production and distribution.

PFE began developing its film strategy in 1992 using a variety of tactics to build its distribution presence in various European territories. These included acquiring existing distributors in the Netherlands, France and Switzerland, set-ting up divisions in Germany and Italy, and a joint venture in Spain. PFE also owned or had affiliated production companies in France, Hong Kong, the Netherlands and the UK, as well as in the US. Stewart Till, President of PFE International, believed that 'the more territories PFE had, the more they could retain distribution profits and the more they could control marketing and dis-tribution themselves' (quoted in Frater, 1997: 14). Producing films on both sides of the Atlantic, by the mid-1990s PFE had become the nearest thing Europe had to a major studio. Yet, by granting the various entities of its network rela-tive independence (including development of local projects), PFE operated a flexible industrial form of organisation particularly well adapted to the Euro-pean context (Creton, 1997).

By 1997, PFE's pan-European structure came close to the distribution strat-egy recommended by the MEDIA programme. PFE's launch of its distribution operation in North America that year was a bold attempt to take on the Holly-wood distributors in their own backyard. However, some of the big-budget films produced by PFE, such as *Panther* (Mario van Peebles 1995 US), *French Kiss* (Lawrence Kasdan 1995 US/UK) and *The Adventures of Pinocchio* (Steve Bar-ron 1996 UK/US/France/Germany/Czech Republic), did not achieve the results needed for profitability. PFE's short-lived ambitions ended when Philips, which still owned 75 per cent of PolyGram, announced it was looking for a buyer. Seagram had purchased MCA, the owner of Universal Studios, and bought PolyGram's music and film operations in 1998. PolyGram's music interests became part of the Universal Music Group, while PFE ceased to be a separate unit and was folded into Universal Studios. The thwarted ambitions of Poly-Gram Filmed Entertainment to become a major European studio highlight the difficulty of establishing a large pan-European distribution network. The case of PolyGram also indicates how, for the global media conglomerates, the film business is a commercial activity like any other.

Current European Expansion

In Europe's film distribution sector, television broadcasters have been active in forging links across European borders. Along with film financing, broadcasters have taken a great interest in theatrical distribution and marketing. France's Canal Plus has been the most ambitious in the 1990s. After setting up its production and sales venture, Le Studio Canal Plus, the French broadcaster acquired a stake in the French distribution company Bac Films and joined with Pathé to create a network of theatrical distribution outlets in several European countries. The two German giants, Bertelsmann and Kirch, have also had involvement in transnational ventures, the former by acquiring theatrical distributors in France and the Benelux through its affiliate CLT-Ufa, and the latter with the creation of Eureka in collaboration with Berlusconi's Mediaset.

At a time when Europe's major media companies witnessed increased concentration of ownership, several independent production companies have felt compelled to establish output deals with distribution companies, including broadcasters, to assure an outlet for their films.[9] As a result, the lines become blurred between independents and the larger groups. In the theatrical distribution sector, the pattern has been for the larger domestic players to absorb smaller existing distributors and then expand outside their home territory. Germany, for example, has seen many of the smaller distributors lose their independence to larger rivals such as Kinowelt. The German conglomerate has an array of alliances and partnerships with production and/or distribution companies in North America (e.g. Alliance Atlantis in Canada), Spain and the UK. Kinowelt was also one of the first European groups to expand its operations into Eastern Europe, moving into Hungary and establishing operations or partnerships in Russia, Poland, the Czech Republic and Romania, where in spring 2000 it opened the country's first multiplex on the outskirts of Bucharest. A similar pan-European production and distribution network involves Germany's Helkon, Italy's Eagle Pictures and Spain's Tri-Pictures.

Independent Distributors

Across Europe the concentration of a few successful titles in the hands of the more powerful companies has led to anxieties among independent distributors. While table 5.2 shows a slight increase between 1996 and 1999 in the number of theatrical distributors operating in Europe, a significant number of small independent distributors are struggling to remain in business as the major groups are now acquiring the more promising art-house titles. For many, the asking price of certain films can be prohibitive. Small distribution companies release only a few titles each year and the level of expenditure on marketing and prints required for a film to make an impact is frequently beyond their reach. With broadcasters increasing their involvement in film financing, independent distributors are no longer able to rely on selling television rights. Many fear this situation is likely to get worse as distribution channels for films increase.

Some independents have already taken their case to the national authorities and/or the European Commission. For example, in Germany during 1999, twelve independent distributors launched a pressure group, Arbeitsgemeinschaft der Unabhängigen Filmverleiher (AUF), to call for regional funds to address the needs of independents and adapt their financial support measures to art-house distributors. In France, with the number of distributed films increasing (607 films in 2000, compared to 350 in 1995) faster than admissions, several independents decided in January 2001 to join forces and campaign to obtain a special status for the independent sector. Calling themselves 'le Club des Cinq', they represented five of the most important French independent distribution companies – including Diaphana, Pyramide and Les films du Losange.

Several of the smaller distributors have started to establish new business partnerships in order to improve their standing in the industry. For example, Eliane du Bois, co-founder and head of Belgian distribution company Cinélibre/ Cinéart, explained the arrangements her company had made with various partners to improve its competitive position:

> Things have definitely changed. It's almost impossible to be a small independent company now. There are so many films on the market – too many – and you have to be able to bid effectively. [. . .] We're now starting DVD releases, thanks to our exclusive partnerships with Belgian distributor Boomerang Pictures and Dutch distributor A-Film and it's A-Video label. We also collaborate with production companies such as Artemis and Les Films du Fleuve (Luc and Jean-Pierre Dardenne) in Belgium and San Fu Maltha's Fu Works in the Netherlands. Studio-Canal is offering us all of its titles. Right now, we're negotiating video and TV

rights. Our partnerships with Studio-Canal in France as supplier and A-Film in the Netherlands as co-distributor gives us more presence in the Benelux (quoted in Johnson, 2000: 12).

Small independent distributors have welcomed European aids for distribution, but the high admission threshold required to qualify for automatic aid does little to prevent the gap from widening between them and the more powerful distributors.

MEDIA claims that 'the distribution of non-national European films outside their own national territories has increased by 85 per cent' over four years (1996–9), a figure inflated by the results of a few British and, to a lesser extent, French films (*MEDIA France Bulletin*, 2000a). While this may suggest the increasing health of Europe's distribution business, overall figures indicate that '[o]f the 500 films produced every year for the cinema in Europe ... only 20 per cent become the object of distribution outside the main country of production, equal to a mere 7 per cent of the market' (Fattorossi, 2000).

CONCLUSION

As more and more European distributors believe the success or failure of a movie at the box office depends on marketing strategy and spending, marketing departments are expanding, and advertising agencies specialising in film promotion are flourishing. Massive marketing campaigns ensure that,

Il Postino (*The Postman*, 1994)

increasingly, positions are affirmed and opinions made before a film is released. Distributors in Europe now openly admit that their marketing costs are increasingly related to production costs. Today, it is not just English-language event movies or the occasional low-budget British film that benefit from the huge spending power of the Hollywood majors. Along with small-budget films, the 'Miramax effect' has helped a small number of non-English-language pictures, such as *Il Postino* (*The Postman*) (Michael Radford 1994 France/Italy), *Kolya* and *La vita è bella* (*Life is Beautiful*), to play in some multiplexes.[10]

A study conducted by *Screen Digest* found strong evidence that '[n]ew and powerful alliances are forming to address the major objective of building a European distribution network' (2000c: 187). However, the most powerful European groups that have emerged have tended to choose English-language productions made for the international market without looking to distribute a broad range of European films.

European distributors are discovering new opportunities through alliances between the Hollywood majors and smaller European distributors, together with joint ventures formed by the smaller independent distributors and the increased range of distribution outlets available for films. Film professionals in Europe are also finding new hope in the priority now given to distribution by the European support programmes. Yet, although national governments and European institutions have pledged to maintain the sector, the demise of smaller distributors remains worrying and there is a strong feeling in the industry that European aids to distribution could be playing a much more significant part in ensuring that European films have greater access to more European screens.

NOTES

1. In France, film professionals, led by film director Patrice Leconte, protested against what they perceived to be unjust media coverage of French genre films (particularly comedies and costume pieces) in autumn 1999. French critics had previously been cleared of an alleged bias towards US films. During 1996, Michel Gomez of the ARP commissioned a report on the press coverage of domestic and American films. The results demonstrated that – in France at least – film critics were not, as alleged, 'Hollywood agents' (Gomez and Monin, 1996).

2. In 1995, the MEDIA Business School estimated that the cost of attending a festival was between US$80,000 and US$100,000.

3. The total includes UPI (Universal Pictures International), the short-lived UK distribution operation of Universal, formed following the 1998 acquisition of PolyGram Film Entertainment by Seagram, the parent company of Universal. UPI ceased theatrical distribution in January 2000.

4. When, in 1998, the two most successful domestic distributors (UFD and GBVI) took 42.74 per cent of the French market (21.41 and 21.33 respectively), 57.23 per cent of UFD's share was for the blockbuster *Titanic* alone (also see note 8).

5. French funding for this category comes from both the Ministry of Culture and the Ministry of Foreign Affairs. In 1997, nine distribution companies received assistance. Altogether, the distribution of eleven films was supported that year, five from the African continent, two from Latin America, one from Asia and three European films (Dubet, 2000: 135).

6. Under the 'Promotion Denmark' scheme, the Danish Film Institute offers around US$50,000 extra help for prints and advertising, but only if the producer has a distribution guarantee. In Sweden, the government also provides funds for actors and directors to promote their films in the country.

7. For a complete survey of the majors' theatrical film distribution arrangements, see *Screen Digest* (1998). In a joint venture, partners are seeking a revenue-sharing arrangement. Joint ventures tend to be used in markets that need a high degree of local knowledge or in less-developed markets as in the countries of the former Eastern Bloc, but they may also be 'a stepping-stone to a subsidiary operation when sufficient knowledge and infrastructure is built up' (p. 35).

8. GBVI is an alliance between Gaumont (France) and Buena Vista, the distribution arm of the Walt Disney Company. France's UFD is the joint distribution venture between UGC (Union Générale du Cinéma) and Fox.

9. An output deal is an arrangement between a production company and a distributor, whereby the producer agrees to supply all the films made by the company to the distributor, who in turn is committed to releasing those films.

10. Miramax has a reputation for aggressively marketing speciality film titles, several of which have been nominated for, and gone on to win, the Academy Award in the foreign-language category.

6

Film Exhibition and the European Box Office

Films are now made available to the public through a range of exhibition windows: theatrical releasing (showing films in cinemas), video/DVD rental and retail, pay television (with subscription services and pay-per-view options), non-theatrical (specialised markets such as airlines, hotels or prisons, which are outside standard theatrical circuits) and free-to-air television. Since the popularisation of television during the 1950s, the arrival of home video in the 1970s, and the spread of cable and direct-to-home (DTH) satellite services from the late 1980s, theatrical exhibition has faced challenges from the consumption of films in the home. However, as a MEDIA Business School report (Sanderson and Lovegrove, 1992: 8) pointed out, theatrical exhibition

> is the initial market in which the bulk of the promotional and advertising budget is incurred [. . .] and all subsequent manifestations of the film, be they on video or television [. . .] and all territories feed off this original promotional activity.

While many films may earn more revenues through home entertainment and television sales than they do in cinemas, theatrical exhibition therefore remains of crucial importance for providing a shop window for the whole commercial life of a film.

Concentrating on theatrical exhibition, this chapter looks at recent admission trends and cinema construction in Europe. General patterns across Europe's exhibition sector are explored, along with particular national developments. As the exhibition business has seen the growth of multiplex construction and the concentration of the market in the hands of a few powerful exhibitors, the chapter also considers the state of the art-house sector in this climate.

CINEMAGOING IN EUROPE

Admissions

Between 1996 and 2000, theatrical admissions in the European Union increased by 136 million (see table 6.1). Europe saw an exceptional increase in admissions during 1998 due to the international success of a single film, the American

Table 6.1 Admissions in Europe (1989–2000)
(Millions)

	1989	1990	1991	1992	1993	1994	1995	1996	1997	1998	1999	2000
Austria	10.2	10.1	10.5	9.3	12.0	12.9	11.9	12.3	13.7	15.2	15.0	16.3
Belgium	16.0	17.1	16.5	16.5	19.2	21.2	19.2	21.2	22.0	25.4	22.8	23.2
Denmark	10.2	9.6	9.2	8.6	10.2	10.3	8.8	9.9	10.8	11.0	10.9	10.7
Finland	7.2	6.1	6.0	5.4	5.7	5.6	5.3	5.4	5.9	6.4	7.0	7.1
France	120.9	121.9	117.5	116.0	132.7	124.4	130.2	136.7	148.9	170.5	153.6	165.9
Germany [1]	101.5	102.5	119.9	105.9	130.5	132.8	124.5	132.9	143.1	148.9	149.0	152.5
Greece	17.5	13.0	10.0	10.0	12.0	8.7	8.2	9.0	11.6	12.4	13.0	13.5
Ireland	7.0	7.4	8.1	7.8	9.3	10.4	9.8	11.4	11.5	12.3	12.4	14.9
Italy		94.8	90.7	88.6	83.6	92.2	98.2	96.5	102.8	118.4	103.5	108.2
Luxembourg	0.5	0.5	0.6	0.6	0.7	0.7	0.6	0.7	1.2	1.4	1.3	1.4
Netherlands	15.6	14.6	14.8	13.6	15.8	15.9	16.4	16.7	18.9	20.1	18.6	21.6
Portugal [2]	12.0	9.6	8.2	7.8	7.4	6.4	12.0	11.5	13.5	14.5	15.2	
Spain	78.0	78.5	79.1	83.3	87.7	89.0	94.6	104.2	105.0	112.1	131.3	135.4
Sweden	19.2	15.3	15.8	15.6	15.9	15.8	14.8	15.2	15.2	15.8	16.0	16.9
UK	87.9	88.7	92.5	98.0	112.6	123.5	114.5	123.8	139.3	135.3	139.5	142.5
Total EU	623.7	609.1	621.2	603.7	689.1	701.2	683.3	708.0	764.0	819.0	808.0	844.0*

Sources: EAO (2001a) (*provisional); *European Cinema Journal* (2001); and MEDIA Salles (2000)

Notes:
1. 1989 and 1990: figures West Germany only.
2. 1989–92: MEDIA Salles estimates; 1993–2000: EAO figures.

blockbuster *Titanic* (James Cameron 1997 US). The renewal and refurbishment of existing cinemas, along with demographic changes which have seen a substantial increase in the number of fifteen- to twenty-four-year-olds – the most regular category of cinemagoers – have played a significant part in raising cinema attendance. The expansion of video and pay television has also contributed to the recovery of the cinema sector by stimulating renewed interest in films. Admissions in Ireland, Luxembourg, Spain and the UK are now higher than at any time since 1989.

During the late 1980s and into the 90s, cinema admissions showed signs of recovery for the first time since the dramatic decline in film audiences in the decades following World War II. In 1960, the residents of the European Community went to the cinema on average 10.5 times a year (London Economics, 1993: 23). By 1992, that figure had dropped to 1.58 visits. Admissions showed some recovery by the end of the 1990s, with EU residents averaging 2.14 visits to the cinema annually (with a peak of 2.17 in 1998). In the EU, Spaniards have maintained their position as the most assiduous cinemagoers (their average attendance was 3.33 in 1999), followed by the French (2.64) and the Belgians (2.23) (MEDIA Salles, 2000: 63). In the whole of Europe, it is the Icelanders who have remained the most prolific cinemagoers, averaging 5.7 visits (8.18 in Reykjavik) per person during 1999, while the Swedes showed the lowest attendance rate (1.81) in Western Europe that year (p. 63).

Since Europe's first multiplex site opened in Britain in 1985, construction of purpose-built multi-screen sites has flourished in the region. In Belgium, Luxembourg and the UK, in recent years multiplexes have accounted for up to three-quarters of theatrical admissions (p. 109). Among the advantages offered by multiplexes, London Economics (1993: 38) cites 'economies of scale in the management of a cinema (not only in terms of staff and technologies, but also in the ability to provide additional services within the same complex)'. The latter normally include free parking facilities, large screens, Dolby sound, comfortable seating, air conditioning, security, advance booking facilities, spacious foyers, sales of related products and catering infrastructures. Multiplexes now characterise the culture of popular cinemagoing in Europe.

Multiplexes have altered the composition of cinema audiences. A survey on multiplex attendance in France conducted by the CNC (Delon *et al.*, 2000) highlighted a split in cinemagoing habits: it found that cinemagoers aged over thirty-five represented 49 per cent of overall admissions but only 28 per cent of the multiplex audience. Under-twenty-fives made up 46 per cent of multiplex admissions and 37.8 per cent of overall attendance. According to the study, younger people preferred multiplexes because of the technical and social supe-

riority such sites offered, which were also the very reasons why many older people tended to avoid them.

Yet the appeal of multiplexes to young audiences is neither universal nor irreversible. In Hungary, the multiplex trend was reported to 'attract older, more highly educated and more upmarket audiences' (Frater, 1999: 11). In the West, new habits and changing demographics are bringing changes in the world of multiplex entertainment. Research shows that in the UK it is women who have most increased their cinemagoing habits. They now account for 51 per cent of the audience compared to 47 per cent in 1989. With an increasing number of screens, together with stable or decreasing number of admissions per screen, several operators have already begun targeting the more mature cinemagoers, a potentially lucrative audience both in terms of wealth and numbers.

In the West, despite large investment in multiplex construction during the 1990s, at the end of the decade, admissions in many countries were showing a slight decline (*Screen Digest*, 2000e: 277). This raises questions about the future role of multiplexes. Loyalty cards are only one of the measures taken by multiplex operators to boost admissions. Others include sales of related products and the use of screens to show events other than film. In comparison to the US, sales of ancillary products in European multiplexes remains limited. However, film-industry professionals fear that, combined with an intensive advertising strategy, sales of ancillary products in theatres could totally change the 'cinema experience' as films cease to be the main draw.

The Importance of Domestic Markets

Putting aside British films which, like Hollywood movies, have little difficulty in reaching international audiences, successful European films achieve most of their box-office success in their domestic markets. Local comedies ranked particularly high in the 1990s in their domestic markets. For example, *Les Visiteurs* (Jean-Marie Poiré 1993 France), *Der Bewegte Mann* (aka *Maybe, Maybe Not*) (Sönke Wortmann 1994 Germany), *Il Mostro* (Roberto Benigni 1994 Italy/France), *Il Ciclone* (Leonardo Pieraccioni 1996 Italy), *Safe Sex* (Thanassis Papathanasiou and Michalis Reppas 2000 Greece) and *Kiler* (Juliusz Machulski 1997 Poland) attracted record numbers of cinemagoers at home.

A study by the European Audiovisual Observatory (EAO, 2000) of the top European films at the European box office revealed that from the European titles on offer, audiences preferred their own domestic productions. In 1999, 77.61 per cent of box-office receipts for European films were earned in their domestic markets. Forty-two of the top European releases saw at least half of their ticket sales come from their domestic audiences; thirteen of these attained

Festen (*The Celebration*, 1998)

all of their sales from their home markets. These thirteen films included *Cosi' è la vita* (Aldo Baglio, Giacomo Poretti, Giovanni Storti and Massimo Venier 1998 Italy), *Pünktchen und Anton* (Caroline Link 1999 Germany), *Muertos de Risa* (*Dying of Laughter*) (Álex de la Iglesia 1999 Spain) and *This Year's Love* (David Kane 1999 UK).

By contrast, domestic admissions only represented 1 per cent of overall admissions for *Festen* (*The Celebration*), the Danish low-budget film of Thomas Vinterberg, and the UK films *East is East* and *Notting Hill* took 8.15 per cent and 27.12 per cent respectively of overall admissions from their home territory. British films frequently perform better in the rest of Europe than at home, making evident the attraction of English-language productions to European audiences.

Measuring Success

Total admissions and box-office gross are only two ways of estimating the commercial value of a movie. An alternative way to gauge a film's success is to examine its print average. In the UK in 1999, the British film *East is East* was released with 257 prints and grossed £10.28 million, giving this FilmFour production an average of £40,010 per print over its first two-month release. This success contrasted with *Plunkett and Macleane* (Jake Scott 1999 UK), which was released on 346 prints and took just £2.7m, an average of £7,803 per print. Also

released in the UK that same year, *Place Vendôme* (Nicole Garcia 1998 France) grossed £182,090, which would seem like mediocre takings, however with only five prints in circulation, this French-language production averaged £36,418 per print.[1]

Another measure of a film's financial success is its budget–admission ratio. In France, some of the most popular and profitable French films of the last few years were made on budgets of under FF25 million: *Marius et Jeannette* (Robert Guédiguian 1997 France) (FF8m, 2.6 million admissions), *La Vérité si je mens* (*Would I Lie to You?*) (Thomas Gilou 1997 France) (FF25m, 4.8 million admissions in 1997), *La Vie rêvée des anges* (*The Dreamlife of Angels*) (Erick Zonca 1998 France) (FF10.2m, 1.4 million admissions in 1998) and *Harry, un ami qui vous veut du bien* (*Harry, He's Here to Help*) (Dominik Moll 2000 France) (FF19m, 2 million admissions in 2000) (*Le Film français* 1998, 1999 and 2001).

CASE STUDY: THE BOX-OFFICE PERFORMANCE AND RECEPTION OF *LOLA RENNT*

For the low-budget *Lola Rennt* (*Run Lola Run*) (see Chapter 2), national awards, an Oscar nomination and European support for distribution helped distributors and exhibitors build audiences across Europe (see table 6.2).[2] A box-office suc-

Table 6.2 *Lola Rennt* – Admissions in the EU (1998–2000)

	1998	1999	2000	Total Since 1998
Austria	79,841	13,973		93,814
Belgium		40,426		40,426
Denmark		8,627		8,627
Finland		2,247		2,247
France		70,145		70,145
Germany	2,057,526			2,057,526
Greece		38,564		38,564
Ireland				
Italy	102,739	5,751		108,490
Luxembourg	8,661	976		9,637
Netherlands		42,211		42,211
Portugal				
Spain			24,641	24,641
Sweden		14,474		14,474
UK		75,976		75,976
Total EU	2,248,767	313,371	24,641	2,586,779

Source: European Audiovisual Observatory <www.lumiere.obs.coe.int>

cess in Germany, the film was released in most European countries and made 1.4 million admissions in the US. With the notable exception of a *Cahiers du cinéma* critic, who dismissed the film as 'a compilation of *déjà vu* effects' (Lalanne, 1999: 97), on the whole critics liked the film, particularly those writing in magazines targeting young cinemagoers. Richard Falcon (1999: 52) explained *Lola*'s appeal in the following terms: 'For all its Teutonic version of *cinéma du look* stylisation, pop-video aesthetics and pumping techno which keeps us breathless, we empathise with Lola, whose lover's pillow talk with Manni about love and death links the three narrative strands . . .'.

However, there were wide variations in the European reception of the film. Speakers at the fourth annual EUROPA CINEMAS Exhibitors' Conference, held in Seville in 1999, identified differences in how the film performed in Belgium, France and the UK.[3] In Belgium, where *Lola Rennt* was released by Cinélibre, Tykwer's film was touted as 'a German *Trainspotting*'. According to Belgian distributor Stephan de Potter, it benefited from 'its selection for the Venice film festival, and a very small guarantee payment which made it possible to spend more on publicity and thus reach a much wider public than the usual cinema-buff crowd'. *Lola Rennt* was presented at as many film festivals as possible and word-of-mouth turned out to be favourable. Moreover,

> it was also screened at sneak previews and presented to the press as the work of a new German and European auteur. It was released in a few multiplexes and in independent theatres, notably those in the EUROPA CINEMAS network. And it was in those theatres that *Lola* found its Belgian public. *Lola* drew 50,000 viewers in Belgium, equalling or outdoing films such as *Kundun*, *Brassed Off*, *The Boxer* and *Ridicule*.

In France, the film's poor performance was blamed on its (French) distributor's strategy:

> 240 dubbed prints were released in multiplexes, targeting the video generation, without any previous presentation to film critics. *Lola* did not benefit from any art-house release and the 'New German Cinema' theme was not exploited as was done in Belgium. [. . .] Directed only towards young audiences, it never found its public.

While today cinéphile magazines are not as influential as they once were, the *Cahiers'* review would have done little to help the film's career on the French art-circuit.

Speaking at the conference, Ian Wild (an exhibitor from Sheffield) used the case of the distribution of *Lola* in the UK to show how important it is for distributors and exhibitors to work together on the marketing of a film. In Britain, *Lola Rennt* was not distributed by an independent, as would normally be the case for European non-English-language films, but by Columbia TriStar. Wild regretted 'the lack of any type of two-way communication on the part of the studio', particularly since he thought 'this could have been a good opportunity to get younger audiences into art-house theatres'. According to Wild, Columbia did not take into account exhibitors' suggestions, as the distributor released *Lola* in the same week as the eagerly awaited American film, *The Blair Witch Project* (Daniel Myrick and Eduardo Sánchez 1999 US), and failed to make the original soundtrack of *Lola* available in record shops as soon as the film came out.

> Independent exhibitors attempted to rescue the distributors' botched strategy locally by organising special promotional activities aimed at media studies and German studies students [with a little help from the Goethe Institute]. However, success slipped through their fingers, for the film and the word-of-mouth process never had time to get established.

In contrast to the UK, *Lola Rennt*'s success in North America made it one of the most successful foreign-language pictures there in 1999. There, Sony Pictures Classics deliberately omitted from its marketing campaign the fact that the film was subtitled.

Table 6.3 Total Number of Screens in Europe (1989 and 1997–2000)

	1989	1997	1998	1999		2000	
				Total Screens	Multiplexes (Screens)	Total Screens	Multiplexes (Screens)
Austria	415	424	424	524	15 (145)	527	18 (174)
Belgium	427	475	497	495	16 (214)	489	16
Denmark	357	320	328	345	2 (26)	350	4 (45)
Finland	345	321	334	362	3 (34)	343	3
France	4,658	4,661	4,773	4,979	93 (1072)	5,103	106 (1,231)
Germany	3,216	4,128	4,244	4,651	87 (841)	4,783	114 (1,079)
Greece	625	280	280	380	4 (47)	380	5 (58)
Ireland	160	228	261	292	9 (99)	315	
Italy	2,373	2,401	2,619	2,839	12 (125)	2,950	21 (217)
Luxembourg	14	26	21	21	1 (10)	25	
Netherlands	426	497	516	561	4 (33)	502	
Portugal	333	322	370	400	7 (78)	420	
Spain	1,802	2,584	2,997	3,343	104 (1,068)	3,505	121 (1,239)
Sweden	1,134	1,165	1,167	1,132	15 (145)	1,131	15
UK	1,559	2,369	2,589	2,825	133 (1,420)	2,954	153 (1,660)
Total EU	17,429	19,938	21,166	22,525	527 (5,580)	23,250	

Sources: EAO (2001a); *European Cinema Journal* (2001); MEDIA Salles (2000); *Screen Digest* (2000f: 279) and (2001c:310)

CINEMAS IN EUROPE
Cinema Sites and Screens
In 1992, almost half the exhibition sector in Western Europe was composed of single-screen cinemas serving sparsely populated rural areas.[4] This is no longer the case today, although Italy and Greece still have a large number of single-screen cinemas, some of which operate only in the summer months. During the 1990s, Western Europe saw a significant increase in the number of cinema screens (see table 6.3). In 2000, France had the highest screen count, with nearly twice as many screens as the UK despite comparable population and admission levels. This variation was largely due to public intervention in France to help maintain cinemas in areas of low-density population. To date, the UK is the only country where more than half the country's screens are located in multiplex sites. This trend has seen cinemagoing in the UK become a leisure pursuit mainly limited to large population centres. Despite warnings of over-saturation in some markets, cinema building continues across Europe.

Even though research by MEDIA Salles (2000) shows that the effect of multiplexes on total admissions is less than generally assumed, in many territories multiplex construction has been a key factor in reversing the decline in cinemagoing seen following the end of the Second World War.[5] The opening in 1988 of the Kinepolis, a twenty-five-screen, 7,500-seat site in Brussels, indicates something of the impact that multi-screen cinemas can have on admissions: within three years, admissions in the Brussels inner-city area had risen by 43 per cent (from 3.5 million in 1989 to 5 million in 1992).

Multiplex Operators and the Internationalisation of the Exhibition Sector
Although multiplex construction has seen Europe's exhibition business become dominated by American and Australian operators (UCI, Warner, Loews, AMC, Village Roadshow), the Sandrew Film Group in Sweden and Bert-Claeys in Belgium were among the first exhibitors to build multi-screen complexes (London Economics, 1993: 37). A decade ago, the degree of internationalisation of the European exhibition sector was small, with the most active move towards internationalisation coming from US-based companies (UCI, MGM, Warner Bros.). When expanding into Europe, the American chains first targeted the UK market, with which they shared a common language and a similar business culture. From their UK-based operations, they went on to penetrate other European countries, usually avoiding direct competition with each other in the same territory. However, outside the UK, US investment in multiplex construction has been limited by the entrenched position of national operators and the nature of national and local government intervention. In the *White Book of the European Exhibition Industry Vol. 2*, a

Table 6.4 Leading Operators of Pan-European Cinema Circuits (2001)
(Ranked by Number of Screens)

	Parent Country	European Territories	Total Sites	Total Screens	Screens per Site
UCI Cinemas	UK/US	7	85	738	8.7
UGC	France	5	82	693	8.5
Europalaces	France	3	80	667	8.3
Village Roadshow	Australia	6	49	483	9.9
Warner Bros	USA	2	37	380	10.3
Greater Union	Australia	3	46	305	6.6
National Amusements	USA	1	17	224	13.2
Kinepolis	Belgium	4	17	219	12.9
Ster Kinekor	South Africa	8	13	152	11.7
Loews Cineplex	USA	3	14	114	8.1
International Theatres	Israel	3	12	108	9.0
AMC Theatres	USA	4	5	100	20.0
Minerva	Netherlands	2	21	89	4.2

Source: *Screen Digest* (2001a: 277)

report by London Economics and BIPE Conseil on behalf of MEDIA Salles, it was observed that:

> Holland, Germany and France, have firm policies regarding development of their cities. Authorities are opposed to the building of multiplexes on the outskirts of cities, on the grounds that this would attract people to the suburbs, thereby increasing the ongoing economic deterioration of the city centres. This is both an economic and a social policy (London Economics and BIPE Conseil, 1994b).

Over the last decade, national operators in Europe have been extremely active in the construction of multiplexes both at home and in neighbouring countries. With high investment costs (building, land prices and regulation requirements), only the larger players have thrived.

As multiplex construction has grown across Europe, over-investment by US chains has created a problem of over-screening for some exhibitors. While European multiplex operators have not experienced the same difficulties, overcapacity in several urban areas has already led to fierce competition, and a number of operators have considered joining forces or have already done so (e.g. Gaumont and Pathé in France under the new entity Europalaces). Despite the increased internationalisation of exhibition in Europe, as table 6.4 shows,

French operators (UGC and Europalaces) are now among the largest European operators of circuits in the region.

NATIONAL DEVELOPMENTS

Exhibition practices vary across European territories depending on:

- the role of public intervention, both in terms of urban planning and cultural policy
- the geographical distribution of exhibitors
- contrasts between urban centres and low-populated areas
- degrees of integration or competition between operators

Contractual arrangements between distributors and exhibitors differ in the terms they set, but the most familiar type of agreement is based on a proportional share of the takings without a guaranteed minimum. It was noted in 1994 that the practice of guaranteeing a minimum had been revived in certain countries (Spain and the Netherlands) but mainly for exhibitors in less populated areas (London Economics and BIPE Conseil, 1994a). Only in France and Belgium does the law fix minimum and maximum levels for film rentals (the sums paid by distributors to exhibitors).

Public Intervention

Intervention by public authorities in the exhibition sector takes several forms:

- investment in the modernisation of cinemas
- subsidies to maintain cinema operations in weaker sections of the market (e.g. rural areas, art and experimental cinemas, non-commercial circuits)
- aid for the purchase and distribution of prints

France operates the most comprehensive and generous system of public support for exhibitors through the redistribution of revenues within the audiovisual sector. Financial support is available to renovate, maintain and create cinemas. Public monies are also used to improve the circulation of national – and European – films in the domestic market or promote their visibility abroad. In the EU, Denmark offers the second highest level of public support in terms of funding per screen (London Economics and BIPE Conseil, 1994b). Local government support is most important in Germany, Italy and the Netherlands, and by the late 1990s, local authorities across Europe were under pressure to maintain – and in some cases, increase – their support to small exhibitors.

Spain reintroduced screen quotas in 2001 (see Chapter 5), despite the protests of exhibitors who objected to the quota system on the ground that it affected their profitability and had the opposite effect of what it was supposed to do (that is, favour the exhibition of EC films).

Belgium

The UK and Belgium were the first European countries to welcome the multiplex revolution. Both countries now have high levels of concentration in their exhibition industries. In Belgium during the 1990s, the upsurge in the number of multiplexes in out-of-town sites was frequently seen as an example of how to reverse the downward trend in admissions. Today, however, the establishment of multiplexes is stagnating (Wolff, 2001: 2). The largest exhibition operator is the Kinepolis group (following the merger of the Bert and Claeys group in 1997). Kinepolis' strategy has been to consolidate and modernise the company's existing circuits, enter into alliances with smaller operators (usually acquiring 20 per cent of their operations), and expand activities outside Belgium.

The UK

In the UK, overseas companies own nearly 60 per cent of multiplexes. These companies include the US-owned multiplex chains of UCI, Warner Village and Showcase, but also the French group UGC (which took over the Virgin circuit in 1999) (Derecki, 2000: 6). However, the British-owned Odeon chain (acquired by Cinven in February 2000) operates the largest number of cinema sites in the country. Public intervention has been limited to the support provided by the British Film Institute for a network of regional film theatres and a small number of municipal cinemas. With competition becoming more intense and operating margins tight, operators have tended to be more conservative in deciding which films to book. Despite the increased number of screens emerging from the multiplex boom that started in the late 1980s and continued into the 1990s, offbeat or specialty product rarely finds a place in multiplex programming (Thomas, 1998: 30). The newly formed Film Council (2000: 27) made 'a proposal for a revitalised cultural cinema network able to act as a circuit'. '[B]ased on the premise that drawing a fixed line between commercial and cultural exhibition is counter-productive and anticipating the arrival of digital exhibition technologies', the proposal aimed to deal with the present 'chronic under-investment in cultural exhibition in England' (p. 27).

Italy

Of the major EU territories, Italy is the most under-equipped in terms of multiplexes. Until 1975, Italy had more cinemas and admissions than the European

Community average. Between 1975 and 1990, admissions dropped from 514 million to 90 million. The number of cinemas fell from 8,000 in the early 1980s, to 2,276 in 1990. Investment was poor and cinema construction slow in a market dominated by regional distributors. The building of multiplexes really started only in the late 1990s. Multi-screen cinemas account for a marginal part of the market (12 per cent in 2000) but several multiplex developers (Warner, Pathé, UGC) are now investing in a number of sites. Most multiplex sites are located in northern Italy (Bodo *et al.*, 2000: 11). To prevent concentration of ownership and ensure cinema operators enjoy equal access to films, antitrust law restricts the number of cinemas that can be run by a single entrepreneur, setting a limit for any company to a maximum of 20 per cent of the total cinemas in operation throughout Italy. This limit is brought down further if the party is also involved in distribution activities (p. 21).

France

In France, the first multiplex theatre was built in 1993, and the three major operators are all French-owned (UGC, Gaumont and Pathé). After a number of cinema swaps between Gaumont and Pathé, the latter almost completely withdrew from the Paris area. Under pressure from independent exhibitors and distributors, the government has introduced legislation both to curb development of multiplexes and to protect small independent exhibitors. As Daniel Goudineau (2000), assistant general director in 1999 of the CNC explained, 'given that multiplexes favour a certain type of film and create competition which also affects promising art-house films', regulations have been introduced to ensure that cinemas adhere to specified programming requirements:

> If a multiplex happens to have a monopoly in a certain area, it is legally required to offer a certain diversity in terms of programming; if a competitive environment already exists, the multiplex has to leave certain films to independents, who themselves must commit to showing subtitled versions, keeping films for a certain amount of time, etc. and may be eligible for special funding. These regulations, which might be compared to a code of good manners between traditional cinemas and multiplexes, are designed to create a strong network of movie theatres throughout the country, as well as to ensure diversity of programming (p. 7).

Boasting 373 cinemas (74,972 seats), Paris retains a privileged position both in terms of the number of screens and range of programming. Introduction of loyalty passes in 2000 caused something of a controversial development in the exhibition sector. UGC was the first circuit to introduce a loyalty card, soon followed by Gaumont, MK2 and Pathé.[6] Competition between the major players and the ambition to increase admissions lay behind the introduction of loyalty cards by exhibitors. However, protests from producers and other exhibitors in the autumn of 2000 led France's Minister of Culture, Catherine Tasca, to intervene and propose new regulatory measures (as well as impose a fine on UGC).[7]

Germany

Like Belgium, Germany has no laws regulating the building of multiplexes apart from the general planning permits that must be obtained from the regional authorities. 'As a result, multiplex expansion has been somewhat chaotic' and 'independent and art-house theatres now depend on subsidies and outside support to stay in business' (Droste-Deselaers, 1999: 7–8).

Spain

Spain's cinema landscape witnessed dramatic transformations in the 1990s. The leading exhibition circuits are now clustered in the cities with the highest attendance. Important exhibition groups came into being, with links to foreign capital and close ties with the distribution sector. Among them are the Paramount- and Universal-controlled CINESA and a joint venture between Warner Bros. and the Portuguese group Lusomundo, Warner-Lusomundo (the Prisa Group holds 33.3 per cent of this circuit). International exhibitors also include Loews Cineplex (through Yelmo Cinemas), AMC and UGC. In the case of the latter, the French group entered the Spanish market in 1998 with a sixteen-screen multiplex in Madrid. However, Spain still has a large number of domestic cinema operators.[8] Local circuits have organised into networks (e.g. CAEC and ACEC), enabling them to challenge the booking power of larger international circuits.

Portugal

In the late 1990s, the opening of new cinemas was almost exclusively carried out by the major exhibitors (AMC, Warner-Lusomundo, Medeia Filmes and Socorama) (Taborda, 2001).

Nordic Countries

In the Nordic countries, the exhibition sector has remained fairly stable, except in Finland where the opening of three multiplexes has resulted in a considerable increase in both the number of screens and the number of admissions. In Norway and Sweden, the Swedish company Sandrews Film and Norwegian exhibitor Schibsted formed Sandrews Metronome Theatres to build multiplex chains in their respective countries (European Commission, 1997: 17).

Table 6.5 Admissions and Screens in Central and Eastern Europe (1994–2000)

		1994	1995	1996	1997	1998	1999	2000
Bulgaria	admissions (m)	12.22	11.40	2.69	2.68	2.33	2.48	2.21
	screens	156	160	154	121	106	191	202
Croatia	admissions (m)					2.73	2.29	
	screens					147	141	
Czech Republic	admissions (m)	12.87	9.25	8.85	9.81	9.25	8.37	8.72
	screens		817	765	747	764	740	700
Estonia	admissions (m)	1.37	1.01	1.00	0.97	1.06	0.87	1.08
	screens	176	214	197	180	173	174	
Hungary	admissions (m)	16.17	14.29	13.85	16.81	14.57	14.92	15.23
	screens	497	504	498	523	605	571	564
Latvia	admissions (m)	1.58	1.02	0.95	1.26	1.40	1.37	1.46
	screens	261	245	137	114	116	119	111
Lithuania	admissions (m)						1.78	2.10
	screens						99	88
Poland	admissions (m)		22.20	21.41	23.70	19.90	26.62	18.70
	screens		759	828	825	841	860	
Romania	admissions (m)	25.95	17.07	12.63	9.45	6.79	4.19	5.11
	screens	411	434	407	441	379	316	293
Slovak Republic	admissions (m)	6.30	5.64	4.85	4.04	4.08	3.03	2.64
	screens		365	341	337	337	342	
Slovenia	admissions (m)	2.70	3.01	2.66	2.50	2.56	1.95	2.07
	screens			100	93	93	88	
Turkey	admissions (m)		12.60	13.02	17.46	22.64	24.84	26.40
	screens		366	381	487	584	694	457
Yugoslavia	admissions (m)					7.22	3.47	3.18
	screens					186	160	164

Sources: *European Cinema Journal* (2001); and MEDIA Salles (2000)

Central and Eastern Europe

The state of film exhibition in the East is very different to that of the European Union. Declining levels of local production since 1990, along with the progressive closure of dilapidated cinemas, has led to a dramatic fall in admissions in most Central and Eastern territories (see table 6.5). Between 1989 and 1998, average cinema visits per person per annum dropped from 6.6 to 1.4 in Hungary, 6.7 to 0.6 in Latvia, and from 8.8 to 0.3 in Romania. This pattern meant that by the end of the millennium, the Bulgarian and Romanian markets had almost entirely collapsed.

Costly investment in multiplex construction is only feasible with international capital, and foreign investment has been rather hesitant. Privatisation efforts have not significantly improved the situation in the region, even though there are variations between countries. Poland has been the fastest-growing market. UCI was one of the first multiplex chains to establish a foothold in Poland and is now targeting sites in the Czech Republic and Hungary in partnership with a Dutch investor. A number of other global exhibitors (Village Roadshow, Cineplex Odeon, Ster-Kinedor) have opened multiplexes – often in partnerships with local companies – and, along with other operators, are planning to set up new sites in the region. Romania saw its first multiplex cinema open on the outskirts of Bucharest in 2000. Development of multiplexes is unlikely to be the key to solving the problems of the film industries in the region. As a 1998 report by the Ministry of Culture of the Czech Republic pointed out, multiple-screen cinemas would only represent solutions for the three or four largest cities in the Czech Republic (EAO, 1998).

ART-HOUSE EXHIBITION
Threats to the Art-house Sector
When the first multiplexes opened, it was feared their development would be detrimental to existing cinemas, particularly in the art-house sector. Yet countries such as Belgium and the UK have enjoyed a resurgence of activity both in mainstream and art-house cinemas. In the early 1990s, the two countries were identified as examples that proved the advent of multiplexes was not necessarily a destabilising factor in the exhibition sector, for 'the market potential created by the multiplexes encouraged the traditional operators to make the necessary investment to raise standards to those of multiplexes' (London Economics and BIPE Conseil, 1994a). It was also noted that the resurgence of cinemagoing in a multiplex's catchment area had 'given the older establishments an incentive to modernise, and in certain cases, to increase their capacity'. However, over recent years, both countries have also seen cinema closures despite protest movements emanating from local residents, and there is little doubt that the increased capacity of the recently modernised houses is also due to the closure of less fortunate cinemas.[9]

Over the last decade, independent exhibitors across Europe have felt squeezed by the tendency of the major industry players to build their own circuits and/or forge programming alliances with smaller distributors. The impact of multiplexes on smaller exhibitors is not only evident in areas of low-density population but also in major cities, even in countries that operate support mechanisms for independents. Smaller exhibitors operating sites are now finding that, in certain regions close to overcapacity, they are in direct competition with multiplex operators who have started to screen art-house product to attract new audiences.

'You are writing a necrology', said Gérard and Sylvain Clochard in an interview in *Cahiers du cinéma* (author's translation, Lequeret, 2000b: 36). The owners of Le Concorde, a four-screen independent cinema in the centre of Nantes (western France, population: 240,000), now feel that they are unable to compete with their powerful rivals who control five multi-screen sites in the same city and think it is too late to take action. 'Independents should have joined forces fifteen years ago. What happened in the food distribution sector and in the music world should have served as a warning to *art et essai* cinema operators' (author's translation, pp. 36–7). Le Concorde–Nantes is not an isolated case in France. Even Paris, a city reputed as enjoying 'the widest menu of films on offer at any given moment to the public in any city in the world' (Allen J. Scott, 2000a: 105) is now being affected.

C. Kantcheff (1999: 21) suggested that anyone who would doubt the priority given to profitability in the multiplex sector should read the following advertisement from the American exhibitor AMC to recruit a manager for their 'megaplex' in Dunkirk (northern France):

> You will welcome more than 1.5 million visitors per year. You will be in charge of all operational and functional aspects, welcoming customers and making sure they are satisfied, recruiting and managing a team of 130 people. It will be your responsibility to make sure that quality programming, turnover, cash flow, marketing, safety and public relations are all met within the allocated budget. [...] You should provide evidence of holding a successful management post in an economic sector where the number of consumers is the main factor of success (author's translation).

Many independent exhibitors, on the other hand, emphasise the cultural, social and educational role of the cinema rather than profitability, seeing their role as programmers rather than managers.

In Denmark, following cinema closures in rural areas and in the smaller cities, the vice-president of the Danish exhibitors' association warned that the Danish Film Institute would be prepared to 'take legal action if the most powerful groups, in order to extend their influence, would start snapping up art-house and other promising European films', as the release of auteur films in multiplexes would be detrimental to independent theatres for they would 'no longer be able to do their work of discovering and showing previously unknown films to the public' (Rykaer, 1999: 6). Norway's cinemas have long been under municipal ownership and control.[10] As international media companies have looked towards expanding in the country, the Norwegian government has examined ways to protect the municipal system from possible privatisation and to help smaller cinemas survive (Mehlum, 1999: 2).

CASE STUDY: *ART ET ESSAI* THEATRES IN THE LATIN QUARTER IN PARIS

In the late 1990s, Carlos Pardo (1997) reflected on the 'mummification' of Paris and particularly the Latin Quarter following the closure of several of cinemas and bookshops. He wrote:

> Since the 60s, it is at the Cinémathèque and in the Latin Quarter that Parisians have been able to enjoy cinephily, the pleasure given by a movie theatre, the

discovery of a cinema different from mainstream cinema [. . .] [They will not be able to do so] for much longer . . . (author's translation, p. 58).

Many of the cinemas that closed in the district were not replaced. Pardo blames this situation on the opening of the fifteen-screen UGC Ciné-Cité in June 1995. Located on the other side of the Seine in the heart of Paris, and at the intersection of several underground lines, the UGC multiplex sold over 1.7 million tickets in its first year of operation. The site became the most popular cinema in the capital by programming a combination of Hollywood or French blockbusters, and *art et essai* films, all shown in their original version. Within two years, the small cinemas situated on the Left Bank in the Latin Quarter had lost between 20 and 25 per cent of their audience.[11] Since then, the UGC Ciné-Cité has added four screens to its Les Halles site in the centre of Paris, and other multi-screen sites developed in the Montparnasse district have only made the crisis more acute for small local exhibitors.

Claude Gérard, the owner of the Espace Saint Michel cinema in the heart of the Latin Quarter, is well aware that in today's commercial environment, multiplexes respond to consumer demand: 'Today's audiences consume films like disposable products. Distributors want to recover the investment as quickly as possible. Multiplexes are the response to the evolution of commercial cinema' (author's translation, quoted in Pardo, 1997: 60). In and around the Latin Quarter, over twenty cinemas have closed down over the last five years. According to Gérard, the UGC Ciné-Cité is not solely responsible for the plight of the small art-house theatres. He also blames the exhibitor Marin Karmitz (see Chapter 2), accusing him of adopting the same unfair tactics as UGC Ciné-Cité.[12] Karmitz regards himself as belonging to the independent sector, with his MK2 cinema chain working around the art-house and neighbourhood-cinema concept, but the recent introduction of a loyalty pass scheme by MK2 may prove Gérard's suspicions well founded.

Gérard does not think the measures taken today by the French government to protect the smaller exhibitors are sufficient to ensure that the cinema that has been in his family since 1912 will continue to exist. He also believes that the current trend of alliances between the independents and the larger groups will eventually lead to the death of the former. In his opinion, associations such as that between UGC and Diaphana – the successful distribution company of Michel Saint-Jean – are doomed: 'they can only help the small distributors/exhibitors for a short while. In the long run, the smaller partners will lose all negotiating power. They will have no choice but to accept the cuts imposed by the groups'.[13]

Strategies and Fragmentation in the Art Sector

Exhibitors in the art-house sector have used a variety of strategies to attract audiences and hopefully retain the niche they have carved for themselves. These include inviting directors, actors and film critics to discuss films, screening retrospectives dedicated to a particular film-maker, or organising special seasons of films originating from a particular country or continent. In the present climate, the independent exhibitors who seem to have the greatest chance of survival are those who either organise into networks of smaller cinemas, as some Spanish operators have, or like Marin Karmitz, can afford to make substantial investments to turn their cinemas into so-called 'artplexes'. A complex of five or six screens, an artplex offers the same technical quality as a multiplex with a different atmosphere (Pintzke, 1999: 5). Artplexes tend to be geared towards the highly educated, over-twenty-five segment of the cinema audience. Such sites are 'social spaces that bank on a variety of formats, lengths and types of films, both national and international, and which also organise special events' (p. 6). Combining theatres with restaurants, cafés or other services, they promote working at a local level and getting involved with the community. In Paris, but also in the larger German and Spanish cities, the artplex strategy is today proving a success.

Despite European initiatives to help build European networks, such as EUROPA CINEMAS (see Chapter 4), the independent exhibition sector remains fragmented. It includes profit-making mainstream and art-house exhibitors, which either operate as small chains or individual concerns. Alongside these ventures are the non-profit, publicly subsidised exhibitors such as the regional film theatres in the UK. These can range from municipal arts centres or town halls showing a part-time programme, to a multi-screen cinema in the centre of a large city (Stafford, 1999: 10). As discussed in the previous chapter, the number of film festivals has grown internationally to such an extent that festival screenings can also be regarded as an important non-commercial exhibition circuit. In addition, most European countries also have film societies. These non-theatrical exhibitors are often the only local providers of non-American fare and, in fact, the only film provision in some regions. However, here too, numbers have sharply declined in recent years.

AREAS OF CONCERN

Programming

In the major European markets, between 200 and 600 feature-length first-run films are now released every year. A small number of these titles are responsible for a large proportion of box-office revenues.[14] For all the speculation that multiplexes would provide additional opportunities for screening independent films, and that growth in sites and screens would lead to the advent of mini-circuits catering for specific niches, till now these possibilities have failed to be realised. One of the most notable exceptions is in the UK where Bollywood films have become so popular with audiences in urban centres with large Asian communities, such as Birmingham and Bradford, that multiplexes have now started screening them. Yet, examining the 1999 situation, Eddie Dyja (1999: 30) asserted that '[t]he overwhelming product remain[ed] that of American mainstream movies aimed at 15–24 year-olds'.

Wide Releasing

The belief that marketing expenditure is important to ensure a film's financial success is now widespread. A few years ago, *Le Film français* exposed the gullibility and/or insecurity of French exhibitors when it was revealed that a front-page advertisement in the trade magazine announcing the immediate release of '1,300 prints' prompted thousands of enquiries from panic-stricken exhibitors who wanted to know the identity of the film receiving such a huge release. They were disappointed when they discovered that the 1,300 prints were only for the trailer to *Bram Stoker's Dracula* (Francis Ford Coppola 1992 US), not the film itself (Guérand, 1993).

Wide-release strategies benefit only a small number of films distributed in any year. In France, in 1999, ninety films were released on 200 prints or more (compared to just forty-four in 1994), and three films – *Astérix et Obélix contre César*, *Star Wars: Episode I – The Phantom Menace* and *Tarzan* (Chris Buck and Kevin Lima 1999 US) – were released on more than 700 copies. These three films were the only titles to achieve more than 5 million admissions that year (9, 7 and 6 million respectively). The following year, French distributor ARP released *Taxi 2* (Gérard Krawczyk 2000 France) across 831 screens and 'was paid back handsomely with a record-breaking £20m in seven days' (Mary Scott, 2000b: 4). Large-budget French-made films in the English language, such as *The Fifth Element*, *Joan of Arc* and *The Ninth Gate* (Roman Polanski 1999 France/Spain/US), were all released on more than 400 screens.

In Germany – Europe's most heavily screened territory after France – Kinowelt launched *Scream 3* (Wes Craven 2000 US) on 830 prints. As Mary Scott (2000b) pointed out:

> Kinowelt is by no means blazing a lone trail. In a territory where 750 prints is the norm for a Hollywood release, Constantin also decided to roll out *Werner – Volles Rooaa* on a super-wide release. The screen count for the German comedy sequel, including interlocking prints, was an eye-popping 970, a similar roll-out to blockbusters such as *Independence Day* (917 prints). [...] Only *Star Wars: Episode I*

– The Phantom Menace has gone out on more prints in Germany, breaking the 1,000 barrier. [...] In the UK, *The Phantom Menace* opened on about 780 screens, *Toy Story 2* on 720 and *Austin Powers: The Spy Who Shagged Me* on slightly more than 700. [...] All three films made a box office killing (pp. 3–4).

With several European films now receiving the same scale of release as US blockbusters, the criticism made by French commentators in the mid-1990s that multiplexes are 'les porte-avions du cinéma américain' (aircraft carriers for American films) may seem partly debatable.

Length of Release

Wide releasing does not necessarily work to the benefit of exhibitors. As Patrick Frater (2000b: 2) notes, 'wide releases mean that audience demand for a film is quickly satisfied and few films stay on screen long enough for the sliding scale of rentals to work in the exhibitors' favour'. In recent years the theatrical life expectancy of a film has been considerably reduced as distributors tend to consider the opening weekend as a key indicator of success or failure, with the effect of subsequently determining a film's future run. This climate has tended to favour mainstream Hollywood releases aimed at fifteen- to twenty-four-year-olds, who represent the major share of the audience in Europe's national markets. This trend can be particularly damaging for European films which rely on word of mouth and good critical reviews to help build admissions.

La vita è bella (*Life is Beautiful*, 1997)

As noted by the European Audiovisual Observatory (EAO, 2000: 93), 'European films in circulation usually take longer than American films to reach their full potential throughout the European market.' They gave the example of *La vita è bella* (*Life is Beautiful*), a film that took three years to sell more than 20 million tickets in the European Union. EAO's analysis of admissions for films distributed in the European Union pointed to 'the systematic failure to show even films considered as being "of universal interest" on a wider basis'. In the past, over a period of a few months or even years, these films managed to filter down into the marketplace. During the 1980s and early 90s, Alain Resnais, Jacques Rivette and Eric Rohmer, the most elitist masters of the old French New Wave, along with Peter Greenaway and other European auteurs, had little difficulty in exporting their artistically oriented films. Thomas Elsaesser (1992) explained the success of Rivette's film *La Belle noiseuse* (*The Beautiful Troublemaker*) (1991 France/Switzerland) by the fact that audiences saw in it 'a qualified but nonetheless comforting reaffirmation of the values not only of Art, but also of European Art Cinema' (p. 21). However, despite a number of retrospectives in several large European cities, it is now on television rather than the big screen where auteur films are more likely to be seen as the demise of the art circuit has greatly affected their visibility in cinemas.

Securing and sustaining exhibition on the large screen has been particularly difficult for films from first-time directors. A French survey (Lamassure, 1996) showed that in 1995, while first features represented 16 per cent of French production, they only accounted for 1.21 per cent of total admissions (p. 14). Of the 293 feature films produced in the UK between 1995 and 1997, 134 were made by debut directors. However, only eighteen of those directors have since made another film (James, 1999). When word-of-mouth fails to develop rapidly, films get pulled from cinemas before they realise their full potential. This would suggest that lack of visibility is a major problem facing new directors in Europe.

Unreleased Films

Research in the UK has shown that, in the late 1990s, between a half and two-thirds of British films did not have a theatrical release within a year of production. As many as 43.1 per cent of films produced in 1997 remained unreleased and, two years later, there remained no plans to show them. Only 15.5 per cent of UK films managed to have a wide release in 1997 compared to 50 per cent in 1984 (Dyja, 1999: 24). In Germany and Italy, the situation is slightly better, yet a third of German and Italian feature films go straight to television or video. France, where only films that have a statutory theatrical release can qualify for cinema funding, should provide a brighter picture. However, in 1999,

French producer Alain Terzian quoted figures according to which, of the 147 French- or majority-French-produced films announced for 1998, between thirty and forty films still did not have a distributor the following year, and of the rest, a third had a minimal release.

CONCLUSION

Continuing investment in multiplex development across Europe indicates that operators believe that theatrical exhibition will survive competition from home entertainment. The larger operators are concentrating their efforts on the creation of major circuits with little interference from the national and/or European authorities. Admissions may have increased, but in most cases, this does not appear to have resulted in a greater choice of films in the multiplexes. In many cases, it has almost had the reverse effect: exhibitors are fighting battles with an ever-larger number of prints for fewer films in order to attract audience attention, creating a situation in which it is increasingly difficult for the vast majority of films to exist.

Domination of cinema ownership by companies combining exhibition with distribution interests has left smaller exhibitors struggling for survival and access to films. At the EUROPA CINEMAS annual gathering of exhibitors in December 2000, a number of delegates expressed the hope that, with the Internet, they would be able to access films directly from producers. The more pessimistic thought there was little chance of this happening while the power of the larger players continues to increase as a result of concentration and integration trends in the industry.

Strategies such as networking arrangements among domestic exhibitors, and European support to exhibitors (e.g. EUROPA CINEMAS), have provided opportunities for smaller operators. In several territories where multiplex development has almost reached saturation point, some exhibitors have started to show a greater variety of films on their increasing number of screens. This situation, along with the development of artplexes, could help the exhibition of European films, even though it will be of little comfort to the small exhibitors who, like the owner of Espace Saint-Michel, Claude Gérard, have little hope of retaining their independence or their theatre. Moreover, at a time when profits, if any, are more likely to come from television, video rental, video sell-through and DVD, the question needs to be raised whether recent efforts to help the theatrical distribution and exhibition of European films may be misguided.

With the industry excitedly entertaining the prospects for digital distribution, whereby films will be delivered to cinemas electronically, cinemas may be set for another heavy injection of capital. A key hurdle to such a development is the conflict between distributors and exhibitors over who should meet the cost of installing the necessary hardware. Only those who stand to benefit are likely to make the investment. If Europe's exhibition sector does see a large-scale move towards digital distribution in the future, it can be anticipated that this change will serve only to strengthen the position of the existing large US and European chains, as they will be the only operators in a position to raise the levels of capital required for the transition.

NOTES

1. See *Screen Finance* (2000b: 7). The trade magazine suggested that a good screen average could be read in different ways: on the one hand it might be viewed as a well-managed release with distributors and exhibitors using screens efficiently. On the other, it could imply that the film might have benefited from a wider theatrical release.

2. *Lola Rennt* received Eurimages support for distribution in Switzerland, where it made 109,379 admissions, and in Romania (8,068 admissions), Bulgaria (3,319 admissions), Poland (11,618 admissions), Hungary and Slovakia.

3. The following quotes are from the English synopsis of speeches given at the EUROPA CINEMAS Exhibitors' Conference in Seville, 26–8 November 1999 (EUROPA CINEMAS, 2000: 10–11).

4. Of a total of 16,621 screens in the twelve EC states, 7,692 screens were housed in single-screen cinemas, 1,271 in facilities between six and seven screens, and 1,048 in cinemas with eight screens or more (BIPE Conseil, 1998).

5. There is no generally accepted official definition of the term 'multiplex', but most analysts today use the term to refer to a cinema that has eight screens or more, and 'megaplex' for a site with sixteen screens or more (MEDIA Salles, 2000: 37).

6. UGC inherited Virgin's Megapass card when it acquired the UK's Virgin cinema chains in October 1999. In France, the UGC deal offered unlimited access to UGC cinemas for the equivalent of the price of two cinema tickets per month.

7. Announced in 2001, one measure was related to the introduction of loyalty cards – should financial losses occur, the more powerful players would have to compensate the smaller operators. Another required broadcasters to invest an additional 0.2 per cent of their turnover in the theatrical distribution of European/national films.

8. In spring 2000, Spanish distributor–exhibitor Lauren Films merged with Cines Abaco and Cinebox. Together they formed a 235-screen circuit called Central de Actividades y Exhibición Cinematografica (CAEC) (*Screen International*, 2000).

9. Eddie Dyja (1999: 41) reported the loss of eighteen sites and 106 screens in the independent sector in the UK in 1999.

10. Municipal control is arranged via a system of local licence. Of the 260 cinemas

operating in the Norwegian market in 1998, 165 were under municipal ownership and control, and 94 were privately owned (*Film&Kino Yearbook*, 1998).

11. In October 2000, Roger Diamantis (2000), the owner of the Saint-André-des-Arts theatre in the sixth arrondissement, compared the UGC–Les Halles to 'a battleship with a long range firing capacity which could reach the Latin Quarter but also further afield, the Bastille district, the Champs Elysées, everywhere ...' (author's translation, p. 54).

12. Interview with Claude Gérard on 1 December 2000 in Paris.

13. Interview with Claude Gérard on 1 December 2000 in Paris.

14. In 1998 and 1999, the top ten films took around 40 per cent of the domestic market, in France, the UK, the Scandinavian countries (Denmark, Norway and Sweden), Poland and the Czech Republic. All were massively released and advertised. In 1998, *Titanic* made history by taking more than 10 per cent of total box-office revenues in four of the five largest European markets. Among European territories, the film made the biggest impact in Poland, where *Titanic* accounted for nearly 24.2 per cent of total receipts (*Screen Digest*, 2000d: 29).

Conclusion

Recent decades have seen Europeans involved in all sectors of the film industry adapting to a rapidly changing world, and many have relished the challenge. Nevertheless, traditions and cultures continue to structure working practices, and Europe's film industries and the European market remains fragmented. Labour costs and technical facilities still vary considerably from one territory to another, even though specialisation and de-localisation have greatly increased in the last ten years. Teamwork still largely occurs along national lines but is also moving towards European and even global configurations. Strongly encouraged by European and pan-European programmes, networking is well suited to the European film industries at a time of rapid transformations. Combining interdependence and power-sharing, networking enables autonomous entities to initiate appropriate strategies together. To a great extent, the future of the European film industries – particularly in territories which play a smaller role in the region's film business – depends on the proliferation and success of these networks. Reporting on the emergence of 'several poles of excellence', *Screen Digest* (1999b: 267) suggested that in the future, 'the film sector within the European Union [might] gravitate around several poles of excellence, with other territories feeding off these poles', but so far this situation has not developed to any great degree.

On the structural level, production remains the key in the European film industry. Despite wide variations in approaches to film-making and film policy, all European countries operate support mechanisms to foster film production. The introduction of tax incentives in many territories has boosted private investment in the industry. Co-financing arrangements, encouraged and supported by MEDIA or Eurimages, have bolstered film production in terms of both output and budgets. A proliferation of television channels in Europe and the boom in the ownership of video and DVD players have also contributed to rising levels of production. New opportunities are also expected with the arrival of low-cost digital cameras, revolutionising the potential for young film-makers to realise their ambitions without relying on funding from the big distributors. Digital technology promises to make it possible to reach wide and narrowly defined audiences at a reduced cost.

In the early 1990s, Coopers & Lybrand identified the failure of the European film industries to effectively feed distribution intelligence back into the processes of development and production as key to the commercial failure of many European films. There is little doubt that Europeans have started to address this issue. It is now widely accepted that the European film industry needs commercial products generated in Europe and 'commercial potential' is now 'given due consideration' (Downey, 1999: 113). Film producers are changing the way they develop projects. For example, an increasing number of production companies are now working on a slate of films rather than raising funding for single projects.

Theatrical exhibition has changed as a result of multiplex building and the renewal of existing cinemas. Admissions have greatly increased, even though Europeans continue to be less frequent cinemagoers than Americans. Multiplexes and home entertainment technologies may be regarded by some purists as having a damaging effect on film culture, but these outlets have given a new lease of life to the European film industries. European initiatives in distribution and exhibition have led to the number of European films distributed outside their country of origin increasing by 85 per cent between 1996 and 1999, bringing renewed optimism to Europe's film professionals.

European film interests developed economic strategies to compete in the international market. Concentration and integration helped companies to achieve economies of scale. Many of the smaller players found advantages by integrating their operations with a larger group, while the larger European players entered into mergers and alliances – frequently with US partners – to reinforce their position in a particular market or to enter new ones. Even though the challenge for European producers, distributors and exhibitors remains immense in the face of the powerful position of the major US studios, there is some evidence that these strategies can benefit the European film industries. Europeans are now making films with entertainment and production values comparable to those of Hollywood, and an integrated corporate structure makes possible the large-scale international distribution strategy that these productions demand if they are to achieve their best returns. The producer of *Lola Rennt* (*Run Lola Run*) believes that even at a national level, 'group strategies are one of the most effective mechanisms to help us [in the German film business] become an industry' (author's translation, quoted in Vital, 2000a: 14). Encouraged by ambitious European producers, a new generation of European film-makers are prepared to embrace the business strategy of the larger players. Like Tom Tykwer, Mathieu Kassovitz or Roberto Benigni, these film-makers choose a genre likely to appeal to today's multiplex audiences (action film, thriller, comedy) but, in the best European auteur tradition, also claim that they make the films they want to make.

Co-financing arrangements, concentration, integration of production, distribution and exhibition activities, increased attention to marketing – all these strategies, reinforced by the arrival of a new generation of creative artists and producers, testify to the current vitality of the European film industry. However, the European box office remains dominated by American films, with US films accounting for an estimated 69.3 per cent of admissions in 1999 and 73.6 per cent in 2000. The distribution and exhibition of European films may have improved over the last few years but the market share of these films has not significantly changed (see table 7.1). In the European Union, the market share held by European films was estimated at 21.8 per cent in 1998 (the year *Titanic* was released), 29.2 per cent in 1999 and 22.5 per cent in 2000 (EAO, 2001b: 6). These shares were heavily dependent on a small number of titles and on the performance of European films in their domestic markets. Each year, a small number of non-English-language films are successful outside their home territories but, as far as European titles are concerned, it is largely British- and other European-produced English-language films that do well across European territories.

Competition has led to the demise of a significant number of small distributors and exhibitors. To strengthen their position, many European players are forming alliances with the US majors. However, this strategy is not without its dangers. Hoskins *et al.* (1997) have emphasised that 'the independent produc-

Table 7.1 Market Share of European Films (Excluding Domestic Productions) (1989–2000)

	1989	1990	1991	1992	1993	1994	1995	1996	1997	1998	1999	2000
Belgium [1]	21.5	19.3	14.7	19.3	16.5	16.2	20.8	10.9	13.4	11.9	18.1	15.0
Denmark	19.4	6.1	4.7	3.4	5.2	6.9	7.4	15.3	13.1	9.1	15.1	
Finland [2]	24.0	12.5	13.0	25.0	20.0	20.0	11.2	15.7	18.6	8.5	15.3	
France	7.8	5.7	10.0	4.7	4.4	8.7	8.4	6.2	10.0	7.6	11.0	6.0
Germany [3]	16.3	5.6	4.0	6.2	3.4	6.5	5.1	8.9	11.5	6.3		
Greece [4]	5.0	5.0	5.0	6.0	19.0	14.0	21.0					
Iceland [5]								6.7	13.0	5.1	10.3	
Italy [6]	12.8	8.4	12.6	14.2	12.4	11.0	11.7	12.5	15.9	10.8	21.7	
Luxembourg	10.0	17.0	12.0	21.0	17.5	15.0	15.1	16.2	28.4	17.7	27.2	
Netherlands	18.2	5.0	3.0	3.0	4.9	7.1	7.5	3.6	10.5	4.1	14.5	
Norway												
Spain	17.7	16.1	20.0	13.2	10.1	16.9	14.1	11.8	17.6	8.5	19.3	7.0
Sweden				5.3	9.4	13.2	11.4	11.9	14.9	8.7	10.3	
UK [7]			1.9	0.8	1.3		6.1[7]			2.6		

Sources: CNC figures for 2000; and MEDIA Salles (2000: 78)

Notes:
1. Brussels only.
2. 1996 and 1997: percentage of admissions.
3. 1996, 1997 and 1998: gross distribution revenue.
4. Including other films.
5. Reykjavik only.
6. Figures do not always include the same number of towns.
7. All films except US films, UK films and UK co-productions.

tion model has advantages of its own' (p. 66), and until now, it is this model that has best served European specificities. The most innovative and culturally significant films have often been productions from small independent producers. Looking at exhibition, Florence Raynal (2001: 13) remarks that 'independent cinema owners maintain a concern to diversify what they offer and to pass on their passion for the cinema by keeping it alive'. Reflecting on the situation in the UK, Blair and Rainnie (2000: 203) believe that throughout the history of the industry, 'independents [who have had alliances with the US majors] have fulfilled a subordinate role in relation to the majors, witnessed by their dependence on American capital and the fragility of their continued existence'.

Following the Vivendi–Canal Plus–Universal merger, current debates in France about the future of the pay-TV company suggest it is not just the UK independents who are vulnerable vis-à-vis the US majors. It is largely on the model of a public/private duopoly (CNC/Canal Plus) within a strong regulatory framework that French cinema has developed over the last fifteen years. As Vivendi Universal extends its involvement in the US film and television business, the group's centre of gravity, whether in terms of management, financial structure or market focus, appears to be moving to the US. This prospect became particularly evident as financial pressures saw the group looking towards selling off its film and telivision interests, with the US television network NBC emerging as the most likely buyer.[1] Many film-industry workers in France fear that the Canal Plus merger may not augur well for the cultural exception the French have been so eager to defend. In a global distribution strategy, France only constitutes a small market among many others, whose future rests on its ability to generate a profit. In this context, what will become of Canal Plus and its support for the French and other European film industries?

For all the talk of creating a European major able to compete with the US studios, such an ambitious project seems more likely today to turn into the creation of a global communications group that will only promote or defend 'cultural diversity' as long as this is found to be compatible with its economic strategy. Given the wide range of activities of the new European conglomerates and their interests in US companies, the extent to which these investments serve the commercial or cultural needs of European cinema remains to be seen. Whether these companies are able or willing to retain European talent in Europe is also a significant issue for the future of the region's film industries.

For several European territories, the very existence of a local film industry has depended on government intervention. Today, government incentives and regulations continue to play a key role in the development of domestic film industries. However, there is a strong feeling among many industry professionals that the argument, often made by public policy-makers at European and national government levels, that public subsidies do not encourage producers to make films with a strong commercial potential, provides the public agencies with the ammunition necessary to relinquish responsibility for continuing their support. The programmes established at European and pan-European levels since the late 1980s have raised the hopes of Europeans working in the film industry that the sector would also benefit from regulation at European level. However, today, European operators are playing the same game as the American majors with little interference from European and/or national legislation, and European regulators are seen as increasingly acting in the interest of the larger industrial/commercial players.

Despite the dynamism of Europe's film industries, there is a growing awareness of the complexity and unpredictability surrounding the evolution of the whole sector. In the new global media environment, film seems to have become a mere pawn in a game of power and domination. Worldwide, a two-tier system is emerging (global–commercial versus individual–cultural) as the gap widens between large and small players. Inflated promotion budgets and the greater number of films in distribution tend to widen the gap between successes and flops, and between the conglomerates and independents.

What has made European cinema unique is that the profitability of the sector remained secondary (Frodon, 1995: 141). Economic considerations now dominate the film business in Europe and many industry professionals and analysts think all this is happening at the expense of creativity (Creton 2000; Frater, 2000a; Roddick, 1998) and cultural diversity (Dubet, 2000; Vivancos, 2000). The European Commission (Commission of European Communities, 1999: 9) states that it is the objective of measures taken at the European level to 'develop the public's knowledge and taste, for work from other European countries, thereby strengthening European cultural identity in all its diversity (multilingualism)'. At a time when public service broadcasters are being accused of renouncing their mandate to support and disseminate productions rooted in cultural distinctiveness and pluralism in favour of commercial populism, Michel Reilhac, the director of the Forum des images in Paris, suggested that:

> European films should be given exhibition and marketing space comparable to that used for films with a big promotional budget, particularly by authorising access to television promotion for independent films alone, whatever their nationality, to offset the steamroller of the marketing campaigns of the large, particularly American blockbuster (quoted in Garbarz, 2001: 21).

Others were calling for the establishment of a television channel solely dedicated to the screening of European films.[2] Pierre Chevalier, head of fiction at the Franco-German cultural channel, ARTE, contends that 'one of the responses to commercial logic is probably to set up, or preserve, other logics: the logic of sensitivity, of difference, of the minority'. He also argues that 'the institutional should become more political, less on the defensive, more assertive of the absolute prevalence of creation over the economy of the market, while soaking up the latter's energy and enthusiasm' (quoted in Garbarz, 2001: 20).

Educational initiatives, such as the Euro Kids scheme, are essential for developing an awareness of, and a taste for, European film. Initiatives of this kind could be developed further.[3] In Article 7 of the Fédération Européenne des Réalisateurs de l'Audiovisuel (Federation of European Directors) (FERA) 'Proposal for a Directive on Cinema', the following proposal was made regarding film education: 'Member States shall ensure that European film lessons are given in the framework of compulsory education as part of an education policy to image [sic]. Lectures on films shall be part of mother tongue teaching, like literature' (FERA, 2000). Further promotion of film education should be a matter of vital concern for Europe's ministries of education and culture.

Europe's film industries have developed their strengths through the combination of public support at local and European levels, attractive tax policies, and competitive film-making infrastructures. These strategies illustrate just how much individual countries are concerned not only with the creation of new jobs at home but also with the social and cultural value of film. Institutions such as the CNC, the Nordic Film Fund, Eurimages and ARTE are today playing vital economic and cultural roles in Europe's audiovisual environment. It is not surprising therefore that many European film professionals continue to insist that film should be recognised as an economic and cultural sector with its own specificity and, as such, deserving of special treatment in order to preserve its future.

NOTES

1. On 2 September 2003, Vivendi Universal entered exclusive talks with General Electric, the parent company of NBC, with view towards a merger of their media assets (Teather, 2003). At the time of publication, this deal still needed agreement.

2. See the proposals made in 2001 by Richard Miller and Henry Ingberg (respectively, the minister of culture and general secretary of the French community in Belgium) (Sojcher, 2000).

3. Euro Kids was launched by MEDIA in 1996 as a scheme to support theatres committed to programming European film for children and young audiences. Currently the scheme involves more than 300 screens in sixteen European countries.

Bibliography

Abel, Richard. (1993) *The Ciné Goes to Town: French Cinema 1896–1914*. Berkeley: University of California Press.

ARP. (1998) *Les Modes de Production Cinématographique en Europe*. Paris: ARP.

Barraclough, Leo. (2000) 'Welcome to Berlin'. *Screen International: Germany in the New Millennium Supplement*, 4 February: 1.

Barton, Ruth. (2001) 'Irish Film Finance'. Paper presented at the European Cinema Conference, 27–9 January, University of Wales, Bangor.

Bateman, Louise. (1999) 'Marketing Movies Matters'. *PACT Magazine*, September: 12–14.

Batz, Jean-Claude in Jean-Claude Batz and Claude Degand. (1968) *Contribution à une politique commune de la cinématographie dans le marché commun*. Brussels: Institut de Sociologie, Université Libre de Bruxelles.

Benhamou, F. (1997) *Les industries culturelles et l'emploi*. Brussels: European Commission.

Berger, Roland. (1993) *Interim Report on the MEDIA Programme*. Brussels: MEDIA.

Beumers, Birgit. (2000) 'The Barber of Siberia'. *European Cinema: An Introduction*. Ed. Jill Forbes and Sarah Street. Basingstoke: Palgrave. 195–206.

Billard, Pierre. (1995) *L'âge classique du cinéma français: Du cinéma parlant à la Nouvelle Vague*. Paris: Flammarion.

BIPE Conseil. (1998) *MEDIA II Programme: Mid-term Evaluation, Final Report*. Brussels: MEDIA and BIPE Conseil.

Bizern, Catherine and Anne-Marie Autissier. (1998) *Public Aid Mechanisms for the Film and Audiovisual Industry in Europe: Comparative Analysis of National Aid Mechanisms Vol. 1*. Paris/Strasbourg: Centre National de la Cinématographie/ European Audiovisual Observatory.

Blair, Helen and Al Rainnie. (2000) 'Flexible Films?'. *Media, Culture & Society* 22, no. 2: 187–204.

Bodo, Carla, Chiara Guerraggio, Fania Petrocchi and Celestino Spada. (2000) *Market and State in the Film Industry in Italy in the Nineties*. Strasbourg: European Audiovisual Observatory. <www.obs.coe.int/oea_publ/eurocine/IT.pdf.en> (accessed 10 December 2002).

Boudier, Christian. (1994) '"My Father": Comment faire d'un père deux coups'. *Le Film français*, 17 June: 4.

Brown, Colin. (2000) 'Marketing Goes Underground in Hunt for Streetwise Youth'.
    Screen International, 28 July: 7.
Caradec, Patrick. (2000) 'La FICAM prend le dossier des aides à bras-le-corps'.
    Le Film français, 15 December: 9.
Chappell, Crissa-Jean. (1999) 'Movie Maid'. *Film Comment*, September/October: 4.
Christie, Ian. (1997) 'Will Lottery Money Assure the British Film Industry?'.
    New Statesman, 20 June: 38.
CNC Info. (1997) no. 265, May, Paris: CNC.
CNC Info. (1999) no. 272, May, Paris: CNC.
CNC Info. (2000) no. 276, May, Paris: CNC.
CNC Info. (2001a) 'La publicité du cinéma en France', no. 279, April: 18–27.
    <www.cnc.fr./b_actual/r5/ssrub1/cp052.htm> (downloaded 20 December 2001).
CNC Info. (2001b) 'La production cinématographique en 2000', no. 280, May.
    <www.cnc.fr/b_actual/r5/ssrub5/bilancine/metho.htm> (downloaded 29 March
    2001).
Collins, Richard. (1989) 'The Language of Advantage: Satellite Television in Western
    Europe'. *Media, Culture & Society* 11, no. 3: 351–71.
Collins, Richard. (1994) *Broadcasting and Audiovisual Policy in the Single European
    Market*. London: Libbey.
Collins, Richard. (1999) 'The European Union Audiovisual Policies of the UK and
    France'. *Television Broadcasting in Contemporary France and Britain*. Eds Michael
    Scriven and Monia Lecomte. Oxford: Berghahn Books. 198–221.
Commission of the European Communities (1999) *Communication from the
    Commission to the Council, the European Parliament, the Economic and Social
    Committee and the Committee of the Regions Concerning a Proposal for a Programme
    in Support of the Audiovisual Industry*. COM (1999) 658 Final. Brussels.
    <www.europa.eu.int/comm/avpolicy/legis/key_doc/legispdffiles/media_en.pdf>
    (downloaded 3 December 2001).
Conter, Elizabeth. (2000) '"Savoir dire non est peut-être l'une de mes plus grandes
    qualités"'. *Le Film français*, 20 October: 14–15.
Coopers & Lybrand. (1991) *European Film Industry or Art?*. London: Coopers &
    Lybrand.
Coopers & Lybrand. (1993) *The Distribution Game*. London: Coopers & Lybrand.
Creton, Laurent. (1994) *Economie du Cinéma, Perspectives Stratégiques*. Paris: Nathan.
Creton, Laurent. (1997) *Cinéma et marché*. Paris: Armand Colin.
Creton, Laurent. (Ed.) (2000) *Le Cinéma et l'argent*. Paris: Nathan.
Crisp, Colin. (1994) *The Classic French Cinema 1930–1960*. Bloomington: Indiana
    University Press.
Dale, Martin (1992) *Europa, Europa: Developing the European Film Industry*. Paris:
    Académie Carat and the MEDIA Business School.

Dale, Martin (1997) *The Movie Game: The Film Business in Britain, Europe and America*. London: Cassell.

Dally, Peter. (1993) 'The A to Z of Film Terminology'. *MEDIA Business File*, Autumn: 28–31.

Dally, Peter. (1995) 'The A to Z of Film Business Terminology'. *MEDIA Business File*, Summer: 35–8.

Danan, Martine. (1996) 'From a "Prenational" to a "Postnational" French Cinema'. *Film History* 8, no. 1: 72–84.

Delmoly, Jacques. (1996) 'Comment: Critics Are Ignoring MEDIA's Ongoing Achievements'. *Screen International*, 10 May: 12.

Delon, Francis, Jean-René Marchand and Joël Thibout. (2000) *Les Multiplexes*. Paris: CNC. <www.culture.fr/culture/actualites/rapports/delon/delon-net.rtf> (downloaded 3 December 2001).

Derecki, Krysia. (2000) 'Overseas Companies Own Nearly 60 Per Cent of Multiplexes'. *Screen Finance*, 21 June: 6–7.

Diamantis, Roger. (2000) 'Et Pendant ce Temps-là, le Cuirassé UGC Tire Toujours'. *Cahiers du cinéma*, October: 54.

Dobson, Patricia. (1995) 'The New Realists'. *Screen International*, 25 August: 21–2.

Downey, Mike (Ed.). (1999) *The Film Finance Handbook Vol. 1: A Practical Guide to Film Financing for European Producers*. Madrid: MEDIA Business School Publication.

Drinnan, John. (2000) 'European Share of US Box Office Lifts to 5.4%'. *Screen Finance*, 21 June: 5–6.

Droste-Deselaers, Claudia. (1999) Untitled. Paper presented at the Fourth Annual EUROPA CINEMAS Exhibitors' Conference, 26–8 November, Seville.

Dubet, Eric. (2000) *Economie du cinéma européen: de l'interventionnisme à l'action entrepreneuriale*. Paris: L'Harmattan.

Duncan, Celia. (1995) 'State Management'. *Screen International*, 14 July: 10–14.

Dyja, Eddie. (1999) 'UK Film, Television and Video: Overview'. *BFI Film and Television Handbook 2000*. Ed. Eddie Dyja. London: BFI. 13–51.

EAO. (1997) *The Film Industry in Belgium*. Strasbourg: European Audiovisual Observatory. <www.obs.coe.int/oea_publ/eurocine/1424.html> (downloaded 11 November 2000).

EAO. (1998) *Report on The Film Industry in the Czech Republic in 1997*. Strasbourg: European Audiovisual Observatory. <www.obs.coe.int/oea_publ/eurocine/00001779.html> (downloaded 11 November 2000).

EAO. (2000) *Statistical Yearbook: Cinema, Television, Video and New Media in Europe*. Strasbourg: European Audiovisual Observatory.

EAO. (2001a) *Statistical Yearbook: Cinema, Television, Video and New Media in Europe*. Strasbourg: European Audiovisual Observatory.

EAO. (2001b) *Focus 2001: World Film Market Trends*. Strasbourg: European Audiovisual Observatory.

EC Documents. (2000) 'New Financial and Banking Instruments For the Audiovisual Media', Brussels, 19 December. DN: IP/00/1489 EC Report.

Elsaesser, Thomas. (1992) 'Rivette and the end of cinema'. *Sight and Sound*, April: 20–3.

Entertainment Weekly. (1999) 'Alterna-Flicks'. 30 July: 38–41.

Eurimages News. (1994). Strasbourg: Eurimages.

Eurimages News. (2000). Strasbourg: Eurimages.

Eurimages Press Release. (2001) 6 March. Strasbourg: Eurimages.

Eurocinéma. (1996) *Les soutiens publics nationaux et européens accordés aux industries cinématographiques européennes*. Brussels: Eurocinéma.

EUROPA CINEMAS. (2000) *Fourth Annual Exhibitors' Conference Report*. Strasbourg: EUROPA CINEMAS.

EUROPA CINEMAS. (2001a) Press Release, March. Strasbourg: EUROPA CINEMAS.

EUROPA CINEMAS. (2001b) Press Release, June. Strasbourg: EUROPA CINEMAS.

EUROPA CINEMAS/EUROMED. (2000) *Guidelines 2000*. Strasbourg: EUROPA CINEMAS.

European Cinema Journal. (2001) 'Screens and Admissions 1997–2000'. 3, no. 2: 2.

European Commission (1997) *The European Film Industry Under Analysis: Second Information Report 1997*. DG X/C. <www.europa.eu.int/comm/avpolicy/legis/key_doc/cine97_e.htm> (downloaded 27 November 2000).

Eyepiece. (1987) 'Financing the dream factory'. March/April: 70–5.

Falcon, Richard. (1999) '*Lola Rennt*'. *Sight and Sound*, November: 52.

Fattorossi, Romano. (2000) Untitled article. *European Cinema Journal*, 2, no. 2: 1.

Feigelson, Kristian. (2000) 'Les enjeux de la délocalisation'. *Le Cinéma et l'argent*. Ed. Laurent Creton. Paris: Nathan. 142–52.

FERA. (2000) 'Proposal for a Directive on Cinema'. Distributed at the Strasbourg European Film Forum, 13–14 November, Brussels: FERA.

Film Council. (2000) *Film in England: A Development Strategy for Film and the Moving Image in the English Regions*. London: Film Council.

Le Film français. (1996) 'Classement des films 1995: La remontée des films français'. 19 January: 35–41.

Le Film français. (1998) 'Le classement des films 97'. 23 January: 53–60.

Le Film français. (1999) 'Le classement des films 98'. 22 January: 43–50.

Le Film français. (2000a) 'Le classement distributeurs 99'. 28 January: 37–47.

Le Film français. (2000b) 'Les coûts marketing des films US baissent pour la première fois depuis 20 ans'. 10 March: 36.

Le Film français. (2001) 'Le classement 2000 des films'. 26 January: 49–57.

Film Industry Strategic Review Group (1999) *The Strategic Development of the Irish Film and Television Industry 2000–2010*. Dublin: Department of Arts, Heritage, Gaeltacht and the Islands. <www.iftn.ie/strategyreport/filmin.pdf> (downloaded 3 December 2001).

Film&Kino Yearbook. (1998) Oslo: Film&Kino.

Finney, Angus. (1993) *A Dose of Reality: The State of European Cinema*. Berlin/London: European Film Academy/Screen International.

Finney, Angus. (1996) *The State of European Cinema: A New Dose of Reality*. London: Cassell.

Forum du Conseil de l'Europe. (1991) 'The European Film Family Grows Thanks to Eurimages', February: 42–5.

Forum du Conseil de l'Europe. (1993) 'Eurimages', September: 41.

Forum du Conseil de l'Europe. (1995) 'Marin Karmitz, Producer on the Warpath', June: 34–6.

Franklin, Anna. (1996) 'Bloc Busters'. *Screen International*, 16 February: 19–23.

Frater, Patrick. (1993) 'Mr Impossible'. *Screen International*, 2 April: 10.

Frater, Patrick. (1996) 'Language Lessons'. *Screen International*, 16 February: 14–16.

Frater, Patrick. (1997) 'European Union?'. *Screen International*, 31 October: 14–15.

Frater, Patrick. (1999) 'Beware the side effects'. *Screen International*, 26 March: 11.

Frater, Patrick. (2000a) 'Creativity takes a back seat as Europeans talk business'. *Screen International*, 1 December: 1 & 4.

Frater, Patrick. (2000b) 'Predators cast hungry eye on weak exhibitors'. *Screen International*, 6 October: 1–2.

Frater, Patrick and Ana Maria Bahiana. (1996) 'Distributors Give Title a Twist for Foreign Turf'. *Screen International*, 19 January: 25.

Frodon, Jean-Michel. (1995) *L'âge moderne du cinéma français*. Paris: Flammarion.

Frodon, Jean-Michel. (2000a) 'Jean Cazès et l'aide aux films'. *Le Monde*, 25 October: 36.

Frodon, Jean-Michel. (2000b) 'Rencontre: M. Poiroux, directeur d'Europa Cinemas'. *Le Monde*, 28 June: 32.

Garbarz, Frank. (2001) 'What future is there for a creative film industry'. *Label France*, July: 20–1.

Garçon, François. (1995) 'Les co-productions franco-italiennes: l'exemple de la Gaumont'. *Paris–Rome, Cinquante ans de cinéma Franco-Italien*. Eds Jean Gili and Aldo Tassone. Paris: Editions de la Martinière. 67–78.

Gili, Jean A. and Aldo Tassone. (Eds) (1995) *Paris–Rome, Cinquante ans de cinéma Franco-Italien*. Paris: Editions de la Martinière.

Glancy, H. Mark. (2000) 'Hollywood and Britain: MGM and the British "Quota" Legislation'. *The Unknown 1930s: An Alternative History of the British Cinema, 1929–1939*. Ed. Jeffrey Richards. London: I.B. Taurus. 57–72.

Gomez, Michel and Sylvie Monin. (1996) *Presse et Cinéma*. Paris: ARP.

Goodridge, Mike and Patrick Frater. (2000) 'Tykwer Goes to Heaven with Miramax'. *Screen International*, 5 May: 1.

Goudineau, Daniel. (2000) Untitled. Paper presented at the Fourth Annual EUROPA CINEMAS Exhibitors' Conference, 26–8 November, Seville 1999.

Goulding, Daniel, J. (1998) 'East Central European Cinema: Two Defining Moments'. *The Oxford Guide to Film Studies*. Eds John Hill and Pamela Church Gibson. Oxford: Oxford University Press. 471–7.

Greffe, Xavier (1997) *La contribution du secteur culturel au développement de l'emploi dans l'Union européenne*. DG X, Brussels: European Commission.

Guback, Thomas H. (1969) *The International Film Industry: Western Europe and America Since 1945*. Bloomington: Indiana University Press.

Guérand, Jean-Philippe. (1993) 'La promotion des films'. *Le Film français*, 2 April: 22.

Hancock, David. (1996) *Mirrors of Our Own*. Strasbourg: Council of Europe.

Hazelton, John. (1996) 'Multiplicity'. *Screen International*, 19 July: 12.

Henochsberg, Jean. (2000) 'Le cinéma à la carte généralisé à Paris avec l'offre Gaumont/MK2'. *Le Film français*, 15 September: 3.

Higson, Andrew and Richard Maltby. (1999) '"Film Europe" and "Film America": An Introduction'. *"Film Europe" and "Film America": Cinema, Commerce and Cultural Exchange 1920–1939*. Eds Andrew Higson and Richard Maltby. Exeter: University of Exeter Press. 1–31.

Hill, John. (1994) 'The Future of European Cinema: The Economics and Culture of Pan-European Strategies'. *Border Crossing: Film in Ireland, Britain and Europe*. Eds John Hill, Martin McLoone and Peter Hainsworth. London: BFI. 53–80.

Hoskins, Colin and Stuart McFadyen. (1991) 'The US Competitive Advantage in the Global Market: Is it Sustainable in the New Broadcast Environment?'. *Canadian Journal of Communication* 16, no. 2: 207–24.

Hoskins, Colin, Stuart McFadyen and Adam Finn. (1997) *Global Film & Television: An Introduction to the Economics of the Business*. Oxford: Clarendon Press.

Ilott, Terry. (1996) 'UK Film, Television and Video: Overview'. *BFI Film and Television Handbook 1996*. Ed. Eddie Dyja. London: BFI. 20–64.

Informations Programme MEDIA. (2001) 'MEDIA II: Français, encore un effort ...'. January: 4.

Iordanova, Dina. (1999a) 'East Europe's Cinema Industries Since 1989: Financing Structure and Studios'. *Javnost/The Public* 6, no. 2: 45–60.

Iordanova, Dina. (1999b) 'East Europe's Cinema Industries Since 1989'. *Media Development*, no. 3: 13–17.

Iordanova, Dina. (2002a) *Emir Kusturica*. London: BFI.

Iordanova, Dina. (2002b) 'Feature Film-making within the New Europe: Moving Funds and Images Across the East–West Divide'. *Media, Culture & Society* 24, no. 4: 515–34.

Jäckel, Anne. (1996) 'European Co-production Strategies: The Case of France and Britain'. *Film Policy: International, National, and Regional Perspectives*. Ed. Albert Moran. London: Routledge. 85–97.

Jäckel, Anne. (1997) 'Cultural cooperation in Europe: The Case of British and French Cinematographic Co-productions with Central and Eastern Europe'. *Media, Culture & Society* 9, no. 1: 111–20.

Jäckel, Anne. (1999) 'Broadcasters' Involvement in Cinematographic Co-productions'. *Television Broadcasting in Contemporary France and Britain*. Eds Michael Scriven and Monia Lecomte. Oxford: Berghahn Books. 175–97.

Jäckel, Anne. (2000) 'Diversity and Pluralism in European Cinema'. *Unity and Diversity in the New Europe*. Eds Barrie Axford, Daniela Berghahn and Nick Hewlett. Oxford: Peter Lang. 229–48.

James, Nick. (1999) 'Absolute Beginners'. *Sight and Sound*, November: 3.

James, Nick. (2000) 'Distributing in the Dark'. *Sight and Sound*, November: 3.

Jarvie, Ian. (1992) *Hollywood's Overseas Campaign: The North-Atlantic Movie Trade, 1920–1950*. Cambridge: Cambridge University Press.

Jeancolas, Jean-Pierre. (1992) 'L'arrangement Blum-Byrnes à l'épreuve des faits: Les relations (cinématographiques) franco-américaines de 1944 à 1948'. *1895*, no.13: 3–49.

Johnson, Mark. (2000) 'Executive Suite: Eliane du Bois'. *Screen International*, 8 September: 12.

Kantcheff, C. in C. Kantcheff and Jean-Pierre Jeancolas. (1999) 'Multiplexes, les McDo du cinéma: Le cinéma sous le rouleau compresseur des multiplexes'. *Politis*, 6 May: 20–3.

Karmitz, Marin. (1994) *Bande à part*. Paris: Bernard Grasset.

Kelly, Andrew. (2000) 'Briefly Encountering Short Films: Reflections on Running a Film Festival 1994–99'. *Journal of Media Practice* 1, no. 2: 108–13.

Kosslick, Dieter. (1996) 'Comment: Europe May Be Getting Infected By Mad Cinema Disease'. *Screen International*, 7 June: 11.

Labrada, Fernando. (1995) 'Training to the Year 2000: Priority for MEDIA II', *MEDIA Business File*, Summer: 10–13.

Lafontaine, Thierry. (1997) 'Un produit de consommation courante?'. *Le Film français*, 18 April: 20–1.

Lalanne, Jean-Marc. (1999) 'Cours, Lola, Cours'. *Cahiers du cinéma*, April: 97.

Lamassure, François. (1996) 'La vie éphémère des premiers films'. *Le Film français*, 29 November: 14–15.

Lequeret, Elisabeth. (2000a) 'Le cinéma enchaîné'. *Cahiers du cinéma*, July/August: 46–8.

Lequeret, Elisabeth. (2000b) 'Le dernier des indépendants'. *Cahiers du cinéma*, October: 36–7.

Lev, Peter. (1993) *The Euro-American Cinema*. Austin: University of Texas Press.

Lewin, Alex. (1999) 'Cool Runnings'. *Premiere*, July: 71–2.

London Economics. (1993) *Retailing European Films*. Madrid: MEDIA Business School Publication.

London Economics and BIPE Conseil. (1994a) *White Book of the European Exhibition Industry Vol. 1*. Milan: MEDIA Salles. <www.mediasalles.it/whiteboo/ wbvol1.htm> (downloaded 2 November 2000).

London Economics and BIPE Conseil. (1994b) *White Book of the European Exhibition Industry Vol. 2*. Milan: MEDIA Salles. <www.mediasalles.it/whiteboo/ wbvol2.htm> (downloaded 2 November 2000).

Low, Rachael. (1997) *The History of British Film Vol. VII: Film Making in 1930s Britain*. London: Routledge.

Martin, John W. (1983) *The Golden Age of French Cinema 1929–1939*. London: Columbus Books.

Meaux Saint Marc, Françoise. (1999) 'Euro Post Sector Effects Change'. *Screen International*, 19 March: 19.

MEDIA England Bulletin. (2001) 'News'. March. London: UK MEDIA Desk.

MEDIA France Bulletin. (2000a) October. Paris.

MEDIA France Bulletin. (2000b) December. Paris.

MEDIA Salles. (2000) *European Cinema Yearbook*. Milan: MEDIA Salles.

MEDIA II Programme. (1997) 'The Union's Support Mechanism for the European Audiovisual Industry'. DG X-D. Brussels: European Commission. <www.europa.eu.int/en/comm/dg10/avpolicy/media/en/home-m2.html> (downloaded 17 January 1998).

Mehlum, Jan. (1999) 'Cinemas in a Changing World: The Norwegian Organisation of Cinemas Under Pressure'. Paper presented at the International Conference on Cultural Policy Research, 10–12 November, Bergen, Norway.

Morris, Mark. (2000) 'Spinning the Web'. *Sight and Sound: Mediawatch*, May: 12–14.

Neumann, Laurent. (2000) 'Depardieu tire à vue sur le cinéma français'. *L'Evénement du jeudi*, 20 April: 10–11.

Nikoltchev, Suzanne and Francisco Xavier Cabrera Blàzquez. (2001) 'National Film Production Aid: Legislative Characteristics and Trends'. *IRIS Plus* no. 4. Strasbourg: European Audiovisual Observatory.

Pardo, Carlos. (1997) 'Multiplexes, opération danger (2)'. *Cahiers du cinéma*, July–August: 58–63.

Pennington, Adrian (2000) 'The Main Draw'. *Screen International*, 13 October: 16–19.

Petley, Julian. (1999) Review 'David Puttnam (with Neil Watson), *The Undeclared War: The Struggle for Control of the World's Film Industry'*. *Journal of Popular British Cinema*, no. 2: 170–3.

Petrie, Duncan. (1991) *Creativity and Constraint in the British Film Industry*. London: Macmillan.

Petrie, Graham and Ruth Dwyer. (1990) *Before the Wall Came Down*. Lanham: University Press of America.

Pham, Annika and Neil Watson. (1993) *The Film Marketing Handbook*. London: MEDIA Business School.

Pintzke, Thomas. (1999) Untitled. Paper presented at the Fourth Annual EUROPA CINEMAS Exhibitors' Conference, 26–8 November, Seville.

Pratten, Stephen and Simon Deakin. (2000) 'Competitiveness Policy and Economic Organization: The Case of the British Film Industry'. *Screen* 41, no. 2: 217–37.

Puttnam, David with Neil Watson. (1997) *The Undeclared War: The Struggle for Control of the World's Film Industry*. London: HarperCollins.

Raynal, Florence. (2001) 'The Cinema's Battle'. *Label France*, July: 13.

Roddick, Nick. (1998) 'Show Me the Culture!'. *Sight and Sound*, December: 14–17.

Rudolph, Eric (1999) 'Production Slate: A Runaway Hit'. *American Cinematographer*, June: 20–6.

Ryan, Michael. (1995) 'Tips on . . . Sales and Marketing'. *MEDIA Business File*, Summer: 14.

Rykaer, Jens. (1999) Untitled. Paper presented at the Fourth Annual EUROPA CINEMAS Exhibitors' Conference, 26–8 November, Seville.

Sadoul, Georges. (1962) *Le Cinéma français*. Paris: Microcosme.

Sanderson, John and Stephen Lovegrove. (1992) *Film Production: Opportunities for Project Finance*. London: MEDIA Business School.

Saunders, Thomas, J. (1999) 'Germany and Film Europe'. *'Film Europe' and 'Film America': Cinema, Commerce and Cultural Exchange 1920–1939*. Eds Andrew Higson and Richard Maltby. Exeter: University of Exeter Press. 157–80.

Schmitt, Anne-Claire. (1992) *Aides à la production et à la distribution en Europe et au Canada*. Paris: CNC.

Scott, Allen J. (2000a) *The Cultural Economy of Cities*. London: Sage.

Scott, Allen J. (2000b) 'French Cinema: Economy, Policy and Place in the Making of a Cultural-Products Industry'. *Theory, Culture & Society* 17, no. 1: 1–38.

Scott, Mary. (2000a) 'European Exhibitors Reclaim Territory'. *Screen International*, 23 June: 19–21.

Scott, Mary. (2000b) 'Print Runs Under Scrutiny'. *Screen International*, 23 June: 3–4.

Screen Digest. (1997) 'Film Production and Distribution: A Shifting Balance'. May: 105–12.

Screen Digest. (1998) 'From Studio to Screen: The Majors' Integrated Strategy'.
    February: 33–40.

Screen Digest. (1999a) 'Perspective'. May: 119.

Screen Digest. (1999b) 'Towards a Single European Market in Film'. October: 261–8.

Screen Digest. (2000a) 'Booming Times for Italian Production'. April: 103.

Screen Digest. (2000b) 'Dutch Tax Break Extended During Review'. October: 293.

Screen Digest. (2000c) 'Film Production and Distribution Trends: Shift in Balance
    Between the US and the Rest of the World'. June: 181–8.

Screen Digest. (2000d) 'Top 10 Films Take Huge Chunk of Global Revenues'.
    January: 29.

Screen Digest. (2000e) 'Worldwide Cinema: Poor Product Fails the Multiplex Boom'.
    September: 277–82.

Screen Digest. (2001a) 'Uneven Pace of European Cinema Development'.
    September: 277–84.

Screen Digest. (2001b) 'World Film Production Increases. Domestic Film Industries
    Post Positive Gains'. December: 377–80.

Screen Digest. (2001c) 'Worldwide Cinema: Key Markets Strong as Global Admissions
    Dip'. October: 309–16.

Screen Finance. (2000a) 'Box Office Revenue of European Foreign Language Films on
    Release in the United States in 1999'. 21 June: 5.

Screen Finance. (2000b) 'Distribution UK: UK-Produced Films Triple Domestic Box
    Office Gross'. 17 February: 6–9.

Screen Finance. (2000c) 'Eurimages Cannot Fine New CEO'. 25 May: 2–4.

Screen Finance. (2000d) 'Screen Averages for UK Films Rise by One-Third'. 8 June:
    6–8.

Screen International. (2000) *Germany in the New Millennium Supplement*. 4 February.

Sight and Sound. (1996) 'The Business'. April: 4–5.

Simonnet, Dominique. (1993) 'Nos images ont une âme'. *L'Express*, 14 October: 42–3.

Söderbergh Widding, Astrid. (1998) 'Iceland'. *Nordic National Cinemas*. Eds Tytti
    Soila, Astrid Söderbergh Widding and Gunnar Iversen. London: Routledge.
    96–101.

Sojcher, Frédéric. (2000) 'Les enjeux du cinéma européen: double discours'. Paper
    presented at the EASS Conference 'Is there a European Model?', 26–8 March,
    Turin.

Sorlin, Pierre. (1992) *European Cinemas, European Societies, 1939–1990*. London:
    Routledge.

Stables, Kate. (1999) 'Information Overload'. *Sight and Sound: Mediawatch '99*,
    March: 2–5.

Stafford, Roy. (1999) 'British Cinema Now'. *In the Picture*, Summer: 6–12.

Strover, Sharon. (1994) 'Institutional Adaptations to Trade: The Case of

U.S.–European Co-Productions'. Paper presented at the 'Turbulent Europe' Conference, 19–22 July, National Film Theatre, London.

Taborda, Maria Joao. (2001) 'The Cinema in Portugal: Public Intervention and Private Enterprise'. *European Cinema Journal* 3, no. 1: 3.

Taylor, Richard. (2000) 'Soviet Union (former)'. *The BFI Companion to Eastern European and Russian Cinema*. Eds Richard Taylor, Nancy Wood, Julian Graffy and Dina Iordanova. London: BFI. 223–30.

Teather, David. (2003) 'Birth of a New Media Monster'. *The Guardian*, 3 September: 19.

Thomas, Marc. (1996) 'Financing Audiovisual Works in France and in Europe'. *Columbia VLA Journal* 20, no. 3: 495–519.

Thomas, Nick. (1998) 'UK Film, Television and Video: Overview'. *BFI Film and Television Handbook 1999*. Ed. Eddie Dyja. London: BFI. 15–57.

Thompson, Kristin. (1985) *Exporting Entertainment: America in the World Film Market, 1907–1934*. London: BFI.

Tunstall, Jeremy. (1977) *The Media are American*. London: Constable.

UK MEDIA Desk. (2001) 'So What Did Media II Do for Us?'. *MEDIA*, November: 4.

Vincendeau, Ginette. (Ed.) (1995) *Encyclopedia of European Cinema*. London: BFI.

Vital, Philibert. (2000a) 'Allemagne: Où va l'argent de la Bourse?'. *Le Film français*, 15 September: 14–15.

Vital, Philibert. (2000b) 'Belle année pour les Américains ... Outre Rhin'. *Le Film français*, 28 January: 16.

Vital, Philibert. (2001) 'Une Sofica franco-allemande est-elle réalisable?'. *Le Film français*, 12 January: 14.

Vivancos, Patrice. (2000) *Cinéma et Europe: Réflexions sur les politiques européennes de soutien au cinéma*. Paris: L'Harmattan.

Waterman, David and Krishna P. Jayakar. (2000) 'The Competitive Balance of the Italian and American Film Industries'. *European Journal of Communication* 15, no. 4: 501–28.

Wayne, Mike. (2002) *The Politics of Contemporary European Cinema*. London: Intellect.

Wildman, S. and S. Siwek. (1988) *International Trade in Film and Television Programs*. Washington, DC: American Enterprise Institute for Public Policy Research.

Wolff, Joachim. (2001) 'Multiplex Operators and Competitive Illusions'. *European Cinema Journal* 3, no. 3. September: 2–3.

Wood, Nancy and Dina Iordanova. (2000) 'Introduction to Eastern European Cinema'. *Eastern European and Russian Cinema*. Eds Richard Taylor, Nancy Wood, Julian Graffy and Dina Iordanova. London: BFI. 1–4.

LIST OF ILLUSTRATIONS

Whilst considerable effort has been made to correctly identify copyright holders this has not been possible in all cases. We apologise for any apparent negligence and any omissions or corrections brought to our attention will be remedied in any future editions.

1 – *Thérèse Raquin* (*The Adulteress*, 1953), Paris Film Production/Compagnie Cinématographique de Lux; 2 – *Czlowiek z Marmur* (*Man of Marble*, 1976), Film Polski/Zespol Filmowy 'X'; 3 – *Underground* (1995), CiBy 2000/Pandora Filmproduktion/Novo Film; 4 – *Lola Rennt* (*Run Lola Run*, 1998), X Filme Creative Pool; 5 – *Joan of Arc* (1999), © Gaumont; 6 – *Dancer in the Dark* (2000), © Zentropa Entertainments4 ApS/© France 3 Cinéma/© Arte France Cinéma/© Trust Film Svenska AB/© Liberator Productions/© Pain Unlimited GmbH; 7 – *East is East* (1999), © Film Four Limited; 8 – *Kolya* (1996), Biograf Jan Sverák/Portobello Pictures Ltd/Ceská Televize/Pandora Filmproduktion/CinemArt/Centrum Ceského Videa/Eurimages Conseil de l'Europe/Centre National de la Cinématograph/Czech Film Fund; 9 – *Le Huitième jour* (*The Eighth Day*, 1996), Pan-Européenne Production/Homemade Films/T.F.1 Films Production/RTL-TVI/Working Title Films/D.A. Films; 10 – *Il Postino* (The Postman, 1994), Cecchi Gori Group Tiger Cinematogra/Penta Film/Esterno Mediterraneo Film/Blue Dahlia Productions/Studio Canal+; 11 – *Festen* (*The Celebration*, 1998), Nimbus Film ApS; 12 – *La vita è bella* (*Life is Beautiful*, 1997), Melampo Cinematografica srl.

Index

Italicised page numbers denote illustrations; those in **bold** indicate detailed analysis; *t* = table